Deeds, Titles, and Changing Concepts of Land Rights

David Ress

Deeds, Titles, and Changing Concepts of Land Rights

Colonial Innovations and Their Impact on Social Thought

palgrave
macmillan

David Ress
School of Humanities
University of New England
Armidale, NSW, Australia

ISBN 978-3-030-64190-0 ISBN 978-3-030-64191-7 (eBook)
https://doi.org/10.1007/978-3-030-64191-7

This Palgrave Macmillan imprint is published by the registered company Springer Nature Switzerland AG.
The registered company address is: Gewerbestrasse 11, 6330 Cham, Switzerland

For Karen, Morgan, and Jared, as ever—and for a good friend, Andy Obermueller

Preface

As we walked across that field in central Kansas and followed a line of old walnut trees toward the thick stands of cottonwoods by the creek, my friend Andy put the point of this book particularly clearly: Our connections to land go deeper—a lot deeper—than what legal or economic theory tell us.

Andy's great grandparents had settled there more than a century earlier. His grandfather and father had carefully tended to those walnut trees in a tough land simply because they liked them and didn't see the need to gain a few more yards to plant. Down nearer the creek, where we spotted some stalks of milo sorghum still standing after last year's harvest, Andy remembered how his dad liked to leave the last few rows of milo standing, for the birds. I could see the swifts and meadowlarks dart across that wide blue Kansas sky as we talked. There had been deer tracks and scat on the dirt road we had slipped and slid along to reach this favorite spot.

Deep connections. Forged long ago by homesteading—that is, securing a place on the land by cultivating it, just as John Locke had said we should. At a time when a horse and wagon would have taken a day to reach the nearest city—Salina, in those days probably numbering just 3000 people—Andy's people had poured heart and soul into this land, breaking the sod (in this part of Kansas, prairie grasses' roots can work ten feet down in the soil), planting it with wheat and beans and sorghum and alfalfa. Over the generations, they made this some of the most valuable land in the state.

That will pose a dilemma for Andy and his sisters. Cool economic logic says sell. Memories say something else. That was Andy's point that day.

I wrote this history of some of the legal mechanics of buying, selling and owning land in settler societies because I keep running into memories like that, and what they tell us about how we think about what is really one of the most important relationships of all: our place on the land. This is a history of ideas and feelings, as much as of law or government or economics. Professor Jennifer Clark, of the University of Adelaide, got me started on this business of, as she puts it, nailing jelly to the wall. David Roberts and Matthew Dillon, at the University of New England (Australia) shared their interest in social history, whether in colonial Australia or Solon's Athens. My friend Bob Evans, of Williamsburg, VA, introduced me to the wonders of courthouse records rooms many years ago at the Daily Press of Newport News, and my good friend and former boss, Marisa Porto, indulged me spending many happy hours in Virginia records rooms digging up investigative stories for the Daily Press. It was trying to understand the collapse and first steps toward recovery in Virginia's blue crab fishery that kindled my interest in conflicts over private ownership and commons, and I am grateful to Professor Linda Ford of the University of New South Wales, Colin Coates of York University and Taylor Spence of the University of New Mexico for their inputs in my first ventures here.

This book is about what my friend Andy reminded me of, from the spot on that pasture where we could look across and above the cottonwoods to the rolling prairie, stretching to and beyond the horizon—the point Robert Frost made, when he told us that the land was ours before we were the land's. It's time, I think, to belong to the land and not just own it.

Armidale, NSW, Australia

David Ress

Contents

CHAPTER 1

Introduction: Mr. Rowle Tries to Secure His Land

Abstract Uncertain of their right to land in what had been promised as a *terra nullius*, settlers in seventeenth century Massachusetts and nineteenth century South Australia pioneered official systems to publicly declare their places on the land. The impulse to do so arose from the shared circumstances of the two colonies—dismay on discovering land was already occupied by indigenous peoples and a desire for ordered settlement. The results—deed recordation at the local courthouse in Massachusetts, state certification of title through a government land registry in South Australia—would become standard in settler societies and in colonies where traditional land tenure did not easily accommodate plantation agriculture, commercial timber harvest, and mining. Both systems would reinforce the coalescing of a fairly wide range of early modern age notions about land rights into a simpler concept that land was most naturally occupied and used via fee simple (absolute ownership) tenure.

Keywords Deed recordation • Land title • Land registry • Settler society • Usufruct • Landownership

In 1675, after some four decades living more or less easily with the English adventurers by the falls of Maine's Great Works River, the ailing Pennacook sachem called those neighbors to his lodge. Mr. Rowle (the only name the

D. Ress, *Deeds, Titles, and Changing Concepts of Land Rights*,
https://doi.org/10.1007/978-3-030-64191-7_1

English leaders of Piscataqua Plantations ever knew him by) wanted to place a deed in the official records of the town confirming that he and his children belonged on what he had always considered his land.[1] He told them he could sense trouble coming and said that he wanted the world to be able to recognize what uncounted generations of tradition had assured his family: a place on the land. To do that, Mr. Rowle asked the town leaders to write out a statement of his right to that land, to have it validated by a public official and then to deposit it in a place where anyone, for generations to come, could inspect it. This was a procedure still new both to Mr. Rowle and to the Piscataqua Plantation delegation, but it was one that two of those Englishmen had arranged some years before when Mr. Rowle granted them some land along the river.[2] Those earlier records are still there for anyone to see, in the first Deed Book of York County, Maine. One declares that that Humphrey Chadbourne had "bought of Mr. Roles … Half a mile of ground" six years earlier. Another, that Mr. Rowle had granted his "Right of the Ware [weir] at the falls of the Great Works River to Chadbourne "except for … so much smale Alewive" as he and his heirs "shall have Occasion to make Use of for Planting." This transaction was carefully described as a grant by bargain and sale—legal terms that do not describe a purchase but that mean a transfer of rights to land without a guarantee that others might also have rights there. A third deed involved a sale of land to Thomas Spencer for £5 of "a Parcell of Land called by the name of Quamphegon." There is no record, however, in the town or county land records of the deed for his own land that Mr. Rowle sought. That deed, if written, was never recorded in the town book. Unrecorded, his children's right to the land by the falls would cease to exist; unrecorded, the way he understood his place on the land and among his neighbors would, too.

Mr. Rowle's deeds were recorded barely 15 years after the first enactment into law of what was then the brand-new idea that land records ought to be the responsibility of the state to validate and make public. They detail a variety of ways for individuals to place themselves on land that is far more complicated than the fee simple (exclusive ownership) that now are validated in public land records in North America, Australia, and many former colonial territories. Mr. Rowle's deeds, for instance, detailed use and access rights for a fishing weir and reserved a portion of that half mile of ground for a cornfield.[3] This was far from uncommon in the first public land records. The first law requiring recording and public access to land records, a Massachusetts Bay Colony statute of 1634, directed town constables to enter into a book "a surveyinge of the howses backeside, corne feildes, moweing ground & other lands" of the townspeople; that is record ownership (frank-tenems) and use rights to such commons as marshy hayfields (moweing grounds) and pasture (backeside).[4] Back in England, land records, whether of ownership or tenancy or use rights, were held privately and were not accessible for just anyone to see.[5] There would have been no need in England—customary rights, routinely passed on from generation to generation, were rarely questioned or transferred outside a family. The need for a manor court or tenant to consult the private records came up relatively infrequently. At the same time, community consensus and custom, confirmed for generations, long had been enough for Mr. Rowle, like his father and father's fathers, to know where he could set his weir in the spring for alewives, which maples he could tap for syrup in the last days of winter, where his wife could plant her corn, beans, and squash come summer and in which stretch of woods he could hunt for deer and set traps for beaver.

In Mr. Rowle's long-forgotten request, then, is a story about how we think about our place on the land and how it has changed. It is a story, too, about power and how it is exercised over people and over natural resources. Mr. Rowle's place by the Great Works River would end up belonging to others, by virtue of the same town records where he had hoped would secure rights to his land for his children. His mistake was not only to rely on others to record his rights. It also was to misunderstand this point: that saying that you belong on the land is not quite the same thing as to say the land belongs to you. Documentation and, even more importantly, public proclamation, tended to obscure that distinction, both with recorded deeds and two centuries later with the innovation in 1858 on another barely settled shore: South Australia's Torrens system of registering state-certified, indefeasible title to land.

The questions, then, are: first, what did the introduction of deed recordation signify about the ways people thought about their place on the land in the early days of imperial expansion across the Atlantic and, second, what did the registration of title on the South Australian model suggest about how those concepts had evolved over the course of the nineteenth century with transformations in thought that new industrial and financial techniques sparked. Both recordation and registration made it easier to express a notion of property and land just taking shape in more formal theories of political philosophers, legal scholars, and political economists: that land was simply one more kind of asset, its value not found from how people lived on it but merely through the price it fetched on the market.

While the idea of owning land is in many places quite ancient, easy commerce in land is less so.[6]

There is this question, too: why did deed recordation and title registration emerge when and where they did, in seventeenth century New England and mid-nineteenth century South Australia? The one was where Puritans hoped to make a new, moral society in what they insisted was a *vacuum domicilium* (empty house) even as they promised to convert its indigenous peoples to Christianity. The other was where English Dissenters sought a new permanent home on lands of the Kaurna, Ngarrindjeri, Peramangk, and Ngadjuri, with the promise (possibly with fingers crossed) that they would not act as other Australians had and treat the land as *terra nullius* (no-man's land). Both shared subtly distinctive features. In neither colony could settlers sustain the myth that they were moving onto land that nobody else wanted. This posed a moral challenge, since both Massachusetts Bay and South Australia were intended to be permanent havens for religious outsiders, unlike the first British ventures in North America or Australia—the overwintering fishermen in Newfoundland, the gold-seeking adventurers of Virginia's Jamestown, and the prison colonies of New South Wales and Van Diemen's Land. In both New England and South Australia, emigrants were supposed to settle in ordered, nucleated groups. In New England, entire church congregations moved together onto lands granted to township proprietors. In South Australia, the official policy was to sell public land (i.e. Aboriginal land) at high prices to encourage clustered settlement around market towns. It was the distinctive situation of those Puritan and Dissenter emigrants—the physical pattern of settlement, the search for a religious haven in a new land, the marginally troubled consciences that came as they confronted indigenous peoples—that, in their minds, demanded the legalistic niceties of official documentation and proclamation of rights. The perceived need to proclaim land rights in both New England and South Australia arose from emigrants' realization that they had arrived on a shore that was supposedly empty of people and free for the taking, only to find that it in fact was not. And if settlement was to be well-ordered, any individuals right to be in his or her specific place seemed essential.

Later waves of imperialists would seize on the comfort of public land records as they encountered societies across the Pacific, in Southeast Asia, and in Africa with land tenure practices that frustrated plantation agriculture and the extraction of natural resources (timber and minerals, in particular). The sense of uncertainty that came with finally accepting that *terra nullius* was not so empty of people persisted. It persisted well after the first few generations of settlers managed to dispossess indigenous people. It persisted, too, even after the force or threat of arms secured imperial control over, for instance, Fiji, the Philippines, Malaya, and East Africa. Uncertainty was why the deed recording Nathaniel and Mary Witcher's sale of the land at Casco Bay, Maine, repetitively declared that they:

> Hath given granted bargained sold Aliened Enffeoffed Conveyed & Confirmed & by these presents Doth fully clearly & absolutely give grant bargain Sell Aliene Enfeoffed Convey & Confirm" to Joseph Maylem "his heirs & Assignes for ever all their right Title Estate Inheritance property possesion claim & demand whatsoever in & unto any Lands Commages Grants Claims & possessions of Land ... Together with all such liberties proffitts previlidges Commoditys & Appurtenances (repeated twice in the deed)

and, just in case that was not enough, that they also "doth hereby Covenant promise grant & agree to & with ye sd Joseph Maylem" that they

> are ye True Sole & Lawfull owners of all ye afore bargained premisses Haveing in themselves full power good Right & Lawfull Authority to sell & dispose of ye same ... & that ye sd Joseph Maylem his heirs & Assignes shall & may henceforth for ever Lawfully peaceably & quietly have hold use occupie possess & enjoy ye above granted premisses with ye Appurtenances thereof free & Clear & clearly acquitted & discharged of & from all & all manner of ... incumbrances whatsoever.[7]

But such floods of words were not necessary in law. They addressed a perceived rather than real insecurity about the status of land in law. "I apprehend that a deed would be perfectly competent, in any part of the United States, to convey the fee" if it simply said one party had sold a particular parcel of land for a consideration, Chancellor James Kent wrote in his basic textbook on American law. Nevertheless, he added, "persons usually attach so much importance to the solemnity of forms ... to make 'assurance doubly sure'." Buyers still wanted a deed of conveyance "surrounded by the usual outworks, and securing respect, and checking attacks, by the formality of its manner, the prolixity of its provisions, and the usual redundancy of its Language," he added.[8] Eventually, state legislatures dictated terms of a short form deed that followed the chancellor's wording. Nevertheless, when Massachusetts acted to authorize its version of a short form deed in 1912, it required a piling on of verbs to describe the sale, as well as separate declarations that there were no other claims on the land, that the sellers had the right to sell it, that they and their heirs agreed to defend the sale if it were ever challenged.[9]

Selling public land (again, what was in fact Aboriginal land) to permanent settlers at a high price was the founding idea of South Australia. Land sales were to finance emigration and encourage a concentrated, town-based settlement that would create internal markets for farm products. The language of a South Australian certificate of title was more concise, just as any notional listing in a textbook of political economy detailing the ways that people might occupy and use land was shrinking—and, importantly, was beginning to focus attention on the power to buy and sell it. The first registered transfers of country land declared that Governor Sir Richard Graves MacDonnell granted land that was to be held by the grantee and "heirs and assigns for ever," the permanency that had been so important for so long in preindustrial societies when tenants. The only way to uproot this permanent planting was to prove errors in the registrar's handling of the document—remedies in equity (i.e. by a chancery judge empowered to order corrective acts) were barred; an insurance fund was meant to compensate anyone who lost land because of a registrar's mistake. The standard language of title certificates soon evolved to declare the landholder "seised of an estate in fee simple;" that is, that he or she owned the land outright, with absolute rights to occupy, use, waste, and—critically—to sell that property.[10] Holding land was no longer something permanent. The idea of a grant intended for the use of an individual and heirs forever had become instead an asset that could be cashed in.

South Australian registration of title to land, meanwhile, would spread. Title certificates would protect investment in sugar and rubber plantations in Fiji, Malaya, and the Philippines, mines and orchards in British Columbia, wheat fields in Saskatchewan, and grazing land in Colorado where the registrar's sweeping authority allowed a landowner to "wipe away all other claims to a parcel of land," and has been "particularly effective … in purging parcels of complex communal rights held by a significant preexisting Native population based on their own customary property systems."[11] Torrens system registration would come to be seen as a way to secure economic development as African, Thai, Indonesian, and Melanesian farmers moved from subsistence to cultivation of cash crops for world markets. But it often turned out to be the path to a quick sale for cash, or the loss of peasant holding because a debt, carefully recorded at the land registry, could not be repaid.[12]

Over time the formulae used on recorded deeds came to memorialize same rights as Torrens system title certificates did. The mechanics differed, however, and in a way that signals a further evolution of thought about the place of people on the land. With recordation, a rights holder—perhaps the buyer of a parcel of land, or the lender financing the purchase—presents a deed or lien detailing the transaction to the clerk of a county court or an elected Recorder of Deeds. The clerk or recorder checks that the filing is complete, collects a recording fee, inserts the filing in a deed book—these days, an electronic file, but traditionally a bulky, cloth-covered book—and updates the indices that allow others to search for and find the record. The record allows anyone who cares to look the opportunity to see who is declaring rights to a piece of land. The deed, that is, becomes a record of transactions between people, and the validity of those transaction is still subject to challenge. Under Torrens' registration system, a certificate of title is a guarantee by the state of the status of land and is held as a public record by an officer of the state. The certificate is deemed by law to be the ultimate proof of ownership. The land, rather than the people who are involved with the land, becomes the center of attention.[13] The certificate makes the land seem like any other financial asset—a share of company stock, for instance. Ownership is the only relationship that makes sense in that context. In a similar way, as recordation evolved to detail financial transactions—mortgages, liens, and unpaid bills—it, too, tended to present land less as a place to occupy and enjoy and more as a financial issue or investment.

Scholarly interest in the two systems generally focuses on either the costs and the relative effectiveness of each in protecting property rights or on their use in the theft of indigenous peoples' land.[14] Economists have asked if title registration enhances land prices, generally accepting that it does; legal scholars debate which approach better reflects the complexities and conflicts of rights on land.[15] Here, my focus is a bit different: what do these documents indicate about the way people thought about their land and others' lands, about their concepts of their rights and the rights of other people on land, about the role of the state in regulating use, access, and occupation of land? Deeds, like Mr. Rowle's and the Witchers' (and like nineteenth century land cession treaties that reserve use and occupation rights to Native Americans), suggest something more complicated than simple ownership was at stake. This seems most clear when considering the first recorded deeds in seventeenth century Massachusetts, and particularly those land records involving the Native peoples of New England, as Chap. 2 will do. The range and complexity of ideas about land and rights to it can be seen in deeds memorializing gift-and-tribute exchanges or regular rental payments between Native Americans and Puritan settlers, as well as deeds transferring of freehold ownership between Native American individuals. Deeds in this period also record a wide range of transactions among the settlers, including purchase and sale, life estates, and rights to commons.

Chapter 3 will argue that the changing language of recorded deeds, evident by the early nineteenth century across the United States, reflected an evolution in the way settlers, the political leaders of settler societies and political economists thought about land. These recorded deeds undermine a longstanding historiographic tradition that conflates land hunger with a hunger to own land and that sees a United States with millions of slaves, tenants, and squatters, and hundreds of thousands of Native Americans pushed from their lands, as a nation where "Americans came to believe that all men should own land"[16] and where "property is central to the way we Americans define ourselves as a people."[17]

Moving to South Australia's introduction of title registration, Chap. 4 stresses how that system, like deed recordation, arose at a time after the first wave of settlement, in places that were deemed to be *terra nullius* or *vacuum domicilium* but that turned out to be not empty at all. The language of title certificates, like the basic idea behind the founding of the colony, stresses fee simple ownership, and South Australians' early, and frenzied, land dealings (like the political economists' writings and land speculation discussed in Chap. 3) will suggest that settlers were increasingly looking at land more as a financial asset that a place where they could live and work and pass on to future generations. Chapter 5 turns to the adoption of the Torrens system in other settler societies as well in colonies like Fiji, where a colonial government intent on both the development of sugar plantations and the preservation of the position of native chiefs, saw a Torrens registration as a way to regulate relations between settler and native. This chapter also explores adoption of registration in the Philippines and Malaysia where the potential conflict of indigenous land tenure and market-oriented agricultural and mineral product arose. In conclusion, Chap. 6 argues that the practice of writing down and then making public a declaration of rights to land would over time help limit the way people understood their rights to land. This process arose when different peoples met and had to confront the question of how, or if, they could co-exist—that is, whether the same land with all its resources might support two different ways of life.

At a time when, whether in seventeenth century Massachusetts or nineteenth century Australia, newcomers might have thought those resources to be virtually unlimited, the answer to that question of confrontation or co-existence was conquest. Now, as we come to understand what the limits to the resources Nature provides really are, questions of who gets to use them and how and what say the rest of us have in that arises anew. What we proclaim here matters. As, indeed, Mr. Rowle might testify. For not too long after he asked to use the records of the new town of Kittery to secure a portion of the Piscataqua Plantation for his family, members of his band of Pennacook people took matters into their own hands: they tried to confiscate Kittery's record book, aiming to remove any evidence that settlers had any title to land and so assure that they could share the land.[18] Like Mr. Rowle, they failed. And any place for their families, too, has vanished.

Notes

1. William Hubbard, *The Indian Wars in New England*, ed. Samuel Drake (Roxbury, Mass.: Printed for W.E. Woodward, 1865 [first published 1677]) Vol. 2, pp. 263–264.
2. Humphrey Chadbourne's 1643 purchase of that half mile of ground from Mr. Rowle and Mr. Rowle's 1646 transfer of the weir were both recorded on 20 March 1649, York County (Maine) Deed Book 1, folio 6; Mr. Rowle's 1650 sale of land to Thomas Spence was recorded 18 June 1652, Deed Book 1, folio 18.
3. Anthropologists' detailed analyses of Native American land tenure and rights describe a variety rarely reflected in the historiography of indigenous dispossession, which focus more on the overt acts of war, land theft and racial prejudice, as in for example David Stannard, *American Holocaust: The Conquest of the New World* (Oxford: Oxford University Press, 1992), although Peter Thomas, "Contrastive Subsistence Strategies and Land Use as Factors in Understanding Indian-White Relations in New England," *Ethnohistory*, Vol. 23, No. 1, Winter, 1976, pp. 1–18 and Emerson W. Baker, "'A Scratch with a Bear's Paw': Anglo-Indian Land Deeds in Early Maine," *Ethnohistory*, vol. 36, no. 3 (Summer, 1989), pp. 235–256; Allan Greer, "Dispossession in a Commercial Idiom: From Indian Deeds to Land Cession Treaties," in *Contested Spaces of Early America*, Juliana

Barr, Edward Countryman, editors (Philadelphia: University of Pennsylvania Press, 2014); Stephanie Fitzgerald, "'I Wunnatuckquannum, This Is My Hand': Native Performance in Massachusett Language Indian Deeds," in *Native Acts: Indian Performance, 1603–1832*, Joshua David Bellin, Laura L. Mielke, editors (Lincoln, Neb.: University of Nebraska Press, 2011) pp. 145–168; and Harold W. van Lonkhuyzen, "A Reappraisal of the Praying Indians, Acculturation, Conversion and Identity at Natick, Massachusetts,1646–1730," *New England Quarterly*, Vol. 63, No. 3, Sept. 1990, pp. 411–25, have done much to detail Native American voices on land rights. The comprehensive review of Western legal thought about Native Americans in Robert A. Williams, Jr., *The American Indian in Western Legal Thought* (Oxford: Oxford University Press, 1990) unfortunately does not discuss Puritan settlers' *terra nullius/vacuum domicilium* views, the way they used land records or the courts to take Native American land or the moral questions they considered. More helpful here are James Warren Springer, "American Indians and the Law of Real Property in Colonial New England," *The American Journal of Legal History*, Vol. 30, No. 1 (January 1986), pp. 25–58; Jean M. O'Brien, *Dispossession by Degrees, Indian Land and Identity in Natick, Massachusetts 1650–1790* (Cambridge: Cambridge University Press, 1997). The fluidity of New England settler views are discussed in Alden T. Vaughan, *New England Frontier, Puritans and Indians 1620–1675* (Norman: University of Oklahoma Press, 1995); David Grayson Allen, *In English Ways: The Movement of Societies and the Transferal of English Local Law and Custom to Massachusetts Bay in the Seventeenth Century* (Chapel Hill: University of North Carolina Press, 1981) and David T. Konig, "Community Custom and Common Law: Social Change and the Development of Land Law in Seventeenth Century Massachusetts," *American Journal of Legal History*, Vol. 18, No. 2 (April 1974) pp. 137–177.

4. *Records of the Governor and Company of the Massachusetts Bay in New England*, Nathaniel B. Shurtleff, editor (Boston: W. White, Printer to the Commonwealth, 1853) Vol. I, p. 116.
5. English courts consistently ruled that records of land holdings, including records of copyhold tenure in manorial courts or held by borough corporations, were private and not subject to inspection, even in some cases by the copyholder unless he or she had a lawsuit pending, see Rex v Allgood 101 ER 1232 (1798), Rex v Lucas 103 ER 766 (1808), Rex v. Tower 107 ER 795 (1815) and Rex v Justices of Staffordshire 112 ER 33 (1837).
6. Robert C. Ellickson, "Property in Land," *The Yale Law Journal*, Vol. 102, No. 6 (April 1993), pp. 1327–1329 points out that 4000-year-old stone boundary pillars in Mesopotamia denoted land ownership. Olivier Delahaye, on the other hand, argues that these views of the central role of

individual land ownership grow from a distinctively American history, in "Some Questions about Land Economics," *Land Economics*, Vol. 75, No. 2 (May 1999) pp. 327–32, as does Harold Demsetz, "Toward a Theory of Property Rights," *American Economics Review*, Vol. 57, (1967), pp. 347–59. Immanuel Wallerstein, *The Modern World-System: The Second Era of Great Expansion of the Capitalist World-Economy, 1730s–1840s* (Berkeley: University of California Press, 2011) sees the ownership concept expanding with metropole-hinterland trade while Karl Polanyi, *The Great Transformation: The Political and Economic Origins of Our Time* (Boston: Beacon, 2011 [first published 1944]) points to the commercialization of agriculture that came with the later enclosure movement in England.

7. York County (Maine) Deed Book 11, folio 2.
8. Chancellor James Kent, *Commentaries on American Law*, 4th edition (New York: E.W. Clayton, 1840) Vol. 4, pp. 461–462.
9. See, for example, California Civil Code Section 1092, cited in Robert Devlin, *A Treatise on the Law of Deeds* (San Francisco: Bancroft-Whitney Co, 1887) p. 157, note 1; Conveyances Act, 765 Illinois Compiled Statutes 5/9. In Massachusetts, "An Act to Shorten Forms of Deeds, Mortgages and other Instruments Relating to Real Property, Massachusetts General Court, Acts of 1912, chapter 502, said the seller did "hereby *give, grant, bargain, sell and convey*" and did "*covenant* that we are lawfully seized in fee," that the land was "free of all encumbrances," and that they "have good right to sell and convey the same and that we and our heirs shall and will *warrant and defend* the same" The italicized words were usually set in a bold, distinctive typeface in pre-printed legal forms; the elaborate language was supposed to condense the usual wording.
10. See for example South Australia Register Book 1, folio 1 grant of 250 acres to William Ranson Mortlock of Port Lincoln dated 12 July 1858; transfer to Richard Andrews of five lots in Hahndorf dated 25 May 1859 and with a notation in red ink canceling the title because of Andrews' sale of the land, with a certificate to the new owner, Adolph Dorney noted as being in Book 8 folio 119; Dorney's certificate, dated 24 May 1859, includes the new standard language that the registration was "pursuant to" a numbered memorandum of transfer, the dates indicating registration and re-registration of land Andrews held but acquired before the registration system started. Within a few years, the retrospective registration of long-held land was less necessary, as with certificate of title for William Hughes' 115 acres in Onkaparinga hundred dated 7 July 1862, issued pursuant to a memorandum of transfer of land granted in 1860 to one Thomas Stodart Book 31, folio 139 or the certificate issued to Peter Cummings on 17 January 1860, book 10, folio 5 for a town lot in Adelaide. Conflicts of law

and custom between settlers and Aboriginal peoples are a focus in Irene Watson, *Aboriginal Peoples, Colonialism, and International Law: Raw Law* (London: Routledge, 2016) who notes that Australian settlers' colonization violated Aboriginal law principles of responsibility to self, community, the land, and the future.

11. Maria Montoya, "Dividing the Land: The Taylor Ranch and the Case for Preserving the Limited Access Commons," in *Land in the American West: Private Claims and the Common Good*, William G. Robbins, James C. Foster, editors (Seattle: University of Washington Press, 2000) p. 130.
12. James Edward Hogg, *Registration of Title to Land throughout the Empire: A Treatise on the Law Relating to Warranty of Title to Land by Registration and Transactions with Registered Land in Australia, New Zealand, Canada, England, Ireland, West Indies, Malaya, etc.* (Toronto: Carswell, 1920), J.R. Innes, "Land Law and Registration of Title in the Philippine Islands, *Journal of Comparative Legislation and International Law*, New Series, Vol. 18, No. 2 (1918), pp. 266–272. Ahmad Ibbrahim and Judith Sihombing, *The Centenary of the Torrens System in Malaysia* (Kuala Lumpur: Malayan Law Journal, 1989), David S.Y. Wong, *Tenure and Land Dealings in the Malay States* (Singapore: Singapore University Press, 1975); Peter France, *The Charter of the Land: Custom and Colonization in Fiji* (Oxford: Oxford University Press, 1969); D.T. Lloyd, "Land Policy in Fiji," University of Cambridge Department of Land Economy Occasional Paper No. 14 (1982); J. Hunter and C. Mabbs-Zeno, "African land tenure," *Agricultural Administration*, Vol. 23 No. 2, (1986) pp. 109–22.
13. This point is stressed in C.K. Meek, *Land Law and Custom in the Colonies* (London: Oxford University Press, 1949).
14. For comparative studies of the two systems, see for example Richard R. Powell, *Registration of Title to Land in the State of New York* (New York: New York Law Society 1938); Myres S. McDougal & John W. Brabner-Smith, "Land Title Transfer: A Regression," *Yale Law Journal*, Vol. 48 (1939) pp. 1125–1151. For the impact on indigenous peoples, see for example Francis Jennings, *The Invasion of America: Indians, Colonialism and the Cant of Conquest* (New York: Norton, 1975); Amy E. Den Ouden, *Beyond Conquest: Native Peoples and the Struggle for History in New England* (Lincoln: University of Nebraska Press, 2005); Stuart Banner, *How the Indians Lost their Land* (Cambridge: Harvard University Press, 2007) or *American Property: A History of How, Why and What We Own* (Cambridge: Harvard University Press, 2011). Beyond New England's settlement, Patrick Wolfe, "Colonialism and the Elimination of the Native," *Journal of Genocide Research*, Vol. 8, No. 4 (December, 2006) p. 388 argues that "Territoriality is settler colonialism's specific, irreducible element" so that "Breaking-down of native title into alienable individual

freeholds" is essential. See also L. Veracini, *The Settler Colonial Present.* (London: Palgrave Macmillan, 2015) and *Settler Colonialism: A Theoretical Overview* (London: Palgrave Macmillan, 2010); Fiona Bateman and Lionel Pilkington, *Studies in settler colonialism: Politics, Identity and culture* (New York: Palgrave Macmillan, 2011); T. Banivanua Mar and P. Edmonds (editors). *Making Settler Colonial Space: Perspectives on Race, Place and Identity* (New York: Palgrave Macmillan 2010), Cole Harris, "How did colonialism dispossess? Comments from an edge of empire," *Annals of the Association of American Geographers*, Vol. 94, (2004) pp. 165–182. State power and its impact on land is the focus for James C Scott, *Seeing Like a State: How Certain Schemes to Improve the Human Condition Have Failed* (New Haven: Yale University Press, 1998), while Roger J.P. Kaine and Elizabeth Baigent, *The Cadastral Map in the Service of the State: A History of Property Mapping* (Chicago: University of Chicago Press, 1992) and Lisa Blee, *Framing Chief Leschi: Narratives and the Politics of Historical Justice* (Chapel Hill: University of North Carolina Press, 2014) discuss the role of mapping.

15. See, for example Thomas J. Miceli, Henry J. Munneke, C.F. Sirmans and Geoffrey K. Turnbull, "Title Systems and Land Values," *Journal of Law and Economics* Vol. 45 (2002), pp. 565–582; Abraham Bell and Gideon Parchomovsky, "Of Property and Information," *Columbia Law Review*, Vol. 116, No. 1 (January 2016), pp. 237–286; Henry E. Smith, "The Language of Property: Form, Context, and Audience," *Stanford Law Review*, Vol. 55, No. 4 (April, 2003), pp. 1105–1191; Charles Szypszak, "Public Registries and Private Solutions: An Evolving American Real Estate Conveyance Regime," *Whittier Law Review*, Vol. 24 (2003), pp. 663–706; Blair Shick and Irving Plotkin, *Torrens in the United States: A Legal and Economic History and Analysis of Land-Registration Systems* (Lanham, Md.: Lexington Books, 1978).
16. William B. Scott, *In Pursuit of Happiness, American Conceptions of Property from the Seventeenth to the Twentieth Century* (Bloomington: Indiana University Press, 1977), p. 4
17. Joseph W. Singer, "Democratic Estates: Property Law in a Free and Democratic Society," Cornell Law Review, Vol. 94 (2009), p. 1010. For more in this vein, see, for example John C. Weaver, *The Great Land Rush and the Making of the Modern World, 1650–1900* (Montreal: McGill-Queens University Press, 2003) and John McLaren, *Despotic Dominion: Property Rights in British Settler Societies* (Vancouver: University of British Columbia Press, 2005).
18. Petition to the Massachusetts General Court, 7 June 1706, Massachusetts Archives Vol. 40, pp. 858–9.

References

Records of the Governor and Company of the Massachusetts Bay in New England, Nathaniel B. Shurtleff, editor (Boston: W. White, Printer to the Commonwealth, 1853).

Register Books 1, 8, 10, 31 (South Australia).

York County (Maine) Deed Books 1, 11.

Banner, Stuart. 2007. *How the Indians Lost Their Land*. Cambridge: Harvard University Press.

———. 2011. *American Property: A History of How, Why and What We Own*. Cambridge: Harvard University Press.

Bateman, Fiona, and Lionel Pilkington. 2011. *Studies in Settler Colonialism: Politics, Identity and Culture*. New York: Palgrave Macmillan.

Den Ouden, Amy E. 2005. *Beyond Conquest: Native Peoples and the Struggle for History in New England*. Lincoln: University of Nebraska Press.

Greer, Allen. 2014. Dispossession in a Commercial Idiom: From Indian Deeds to Land Cession Treaties. In *Contested Spaces of Early America*, ed. Juliana Barr and Edward Countryman, 69–93. Philadelphia: University of Pennsylvania Press.

Hogg, James Edward. 1920. *Registration of Title to Land Throughout the Empire: A Treatise on the Law Relating to Warranty of Title to Land by Registration and Transactions with Registered Land in Australia, New Zealand, Canada, England, Ireland, West Indies, Malaya, etc.* Carswell: Toronto.

Hubbard, William. 1865 [1677]. *The Indian Wars in New England*, ed. Samuel Drake. Roxbury: Printed for W.E. Woodward.

Hunter, J., and C. Mabbs-Zeno. 1986. African Land Tenure. *Agricultural Administration* 23 (2): 109–122.

Ibbrahim, Ahmad, and Judith Sihombing. 1989. *The Centenary of the Torrens System in Malaysia*. Kuala Lumpur: Malayan Law Journal.

Innes, J.T. 1918. Land Law and Registration of Title in the Philippine Islands. *Journal of Comparative Legislation and International Law, New Series* 18 (2): 266–272.

Jennings, Francis. 1975. *The Invasion of America: Indians, Colonialism and the Cant of Conquest*. New York: Norton.

Kaine, Roger J.P., and Elizabeth Baigent. 1992. *The Cadastral Map in the Service of the State: A History of Property Mapping*. Chicago: University of Chicago Press.

Kent, James. 1840. *Commentaries on American Law*. 4th ed. New York: E.W. Clayton.

Konig, David Thomas. 1974. Community Custom and the Common Law: Social Change and the Development of Land Law in Seventeenth-Century Massachusetts. *The American Journal of Legal History* 18 (2): 137–177.

Libecap, Gary D., Dean Lueck, and Trevor O'Grady. 2011. Large-Scale Institutional Changes: Land Demarcation in the British Empire. *The Journal of Law & Economics* 54 (4): s-295–s-327.

Mar, T. Banivanua, and P. Edmonds, eds. 2010. *Making Settler Colonial Space: Perspectives on Race, Place and Identity.* New York: Palgrave Macmillan.

McDougal, Myres S., and John W. Brabner-Smith. 1939. Land Title Transfer: A Regression. *Yale Law Journal* 48: 1125–1151.

McLaren, John. 2005. *Despotic Dominion: Property Rights in British Settler Societies.* Vancouver: University of British Columbia Press.

Meek, C.K. 1949. *Land Law and Custom in the Colonies.* London: Oxford University Press.

Miceli, Thomas J., Henry J. Munneke, C.F. Sirmans, and Geoffrey K. Turnbull. 2002. Title Systems and Land Values. *Journal of Law and Economics* 45: 565–582.

Montoya, Maria. 2000. Dividing the Land: The Taylor Ranch and the Case for Preserving the Limited Access Commons. In *Land in the American West: Private Claims and the Common Good*, ed. William G. Robbins and James C. Foster, 121–140. Seattle: University of Washington Press.

North, Douglass. 1990. *Institutions, Institutional Change and Economic Performance.* Cambridge: Cambridge University Press.

O'Brien, Jean. 2003. *Dispossession by Degrees: Indian Land and Identity in Natick, Massachusetts, 1650–1790.* Lincoln: University of Nebraska Press.

Parsons, Angas, and A.L. Campbell. 1936. The South Australian Centenary of Legislation. *Journal of Comparative Legislation and International Law* 18 (1): 21–39.

Peacock, John. 1984. Principles and Effects of Puritan Appropriation of Indian Land and Labor. *Ethnohistory* 31 (1): 39–44.

Pike, Douglas. 1961. Introduction of the Real Property Act in South Australia. *Adelaide Law Review* 1 (2): 169–189.

Polanyi, Karl. 2011. *The Great Transformation: The Political and Economic Origins of Our Time.* Boston: Beacon. [first published 1944].

Powell, Richard. 1938. *Registration of Title to Land in the State of New York.* New York: New York Law Society.

Ruoff, Theodore. 1957. *An Englishman Looks at the Torrens System: Being Some Provocative Essays on the Operation of the System after One Hundred Years.* Sydney: Law Book Company of Australia.

Scott, William. 1977. *In Pursuit of Happiness, American Conceptions of Property from the Seventeenth to the Twentieth Century.* Bloomington: Indiana University Press.

Shick, Blair, and Irving Plotkin. 1978. *Torrens in the United States: A Legal and Economic History and Analysis of Land-Registration Systems.* Lanham: Lexington Books.

Simpson, S. Rowton. 1967. New Land Law in Malawi. *Journal of Administration Overseas* 6 (4): 221–228.

———. 1976. *Land Law and Registration*. Cambridge: Cambridge University Press.

Smith, Henry E. 2003. The Language of Property: Form, Context, and Audience. *Stanford Law Review* 55 (4): 1105–1191.

Springer, James Warren. 1986. American Indians and the Law of Real Property in Colonial New England. *The American Journal of Legal History* 30 (1): 25–58.

Stackpole, Everett S. 1903. *Old Kittery and Her Families*. Lewiston: Lewiston Journal.

Stein, R. 1981. Sir Robert Richard Torrens and the Introduction of the Torrens System. *Journal of the Royal Australian Historical Society* 67: 119–131.

Stein, R., and M. Stone. 1991. *Torrens Title*. Sydney: Butterworths.

Szypszak, Charles. 2003. Public Registries and Private Solutions: An Evolving American Real Estate Conveyance Regime. *Whittier Law Review* 24: 663–706.

Vaughan, Alden. 1979. *New England Frontier: Puritans and Indians 1620–1675*. New York: Norton.

Veracini, L. 2010. *Settler Colonialism: A Theoretical Overview*. London: Palgrave Macmillan.

———. 2015. *The Settler Colonial Present*. London: Palgrave Macmillan.

Whalan, Douglas. 1982. *The Torrens System in Australia*. Sydney: Law Book Company.

Wolfe, Patrick. 2001. Land, Labor, and Difference: Elementary Structures of Race. *The American Historical Review* 106 (3): 866–905.

Wong, David S.Y. 1975. *Tenure and Land Dealings in the Malay States*. Singapore: Singapore University Press.

CHAPTER 2

Massachusetts: Going to the Court House

Abstract The first recorded deeds, detailing land transactions between Puritan emigrants to Massachusetts and between those settlers and the Native peoples of New England agreements reflect a wide range of ideas about land within each community. While Puritan leaders claimed the land was *terra nullius*, it was clear that it was not, and uncertainty over their right to be on the land, as well as the need to make clear exact what rights of occupation and use they had led them to decide their new society needed a way for a public declaration of the status of land: recordation of deeds and other land rights documents by a town clerk or in the local court house. Native Americans, too, felt a need to do so, though this did not prevent their dispossession, as the land deeds of various Pennacook, Massachusett, and Wampanoag individuals makes clear.

Keywords Deed recordation • *Terra nullius* • Usufruct • Landownership • Commons • Massachusetts Bay Colony • Native Americans

The Piscataqua Plantation's registrar, Basil Parker, recorded the community's first land record in 1647, 13 years after the Massachusetts Bay Colony's General Court first ordered towns to keep records of land holdings. It was also five years before the Plantation itself formally became part

D. Ress, *Deeds, Titles, and Changing Concepts of Land Rights*,
https://doi.org/10.1007/978-3-030-64191-7_2

of the Bay Colony. The community's English settlers had noticed the Massachusetts Bay and Plymouth innovations and chose to adopt the practice without being compelled to. They liked the idea, and not only because they thought it could make their purchases of Native people's land more secure. It was not just ownership of land that recordation secured. That first deed, for instance, was between two English brothers-in-law. In it, James Treworgy said he "doe fully, freely & absolutely, grant, bargain, sell, assign & set over … all my Lands, Houses, Goods Chattals, Fish, Fishing Craft, Botes & all other Things to the Fishing Trade belonging."[1] Mr. Rowle used a recorded deed to secure his right to keep using his weir, while the same document secured for Humphrey Chadbourne a continued right to use the falls by the weir to power what was then a quarter-century-old grist mill. When John Andrews recorded the sale of his house, he made a point of declaring that "some others" would still have rights to a meadow and "Rough Ground" for cutting timber, tapping springs "or other Priviledges that other Planters hath had and doth enjoy." Francis Champernowne's sale of a house and half interest in an island to Paul White for £200 included the use rights to a meadow and woods and Champernowne's request to place 15 hogs on the island in return for the right to take half their offspring every year. In their recorded deed granting Nicholas Shapleigh the right to use Sturgeon Creek to power a sawmill, John Hord, Nicholas Frost, and Jeremy Sheares (the latter two were illiterate) also granted a right to cut "all the Timber both Pine and Oak" on the north side of the creek, while Edward Godfrey celebrated his son Oliver's wedding in England with a grant of a house, barn, gardens, and grounds at Point Bollogue as well as his interest in the commons at an island used for fishing. Oliver never ventured to live in Maine.[2]

Deed recordation, that is, was the practical way to set rules for using and occupying land when people were relative strangers to one another and had no traditions about rights to land in common, whether they were English settlers confronting Native Americans, or Englishmen thrown together on a New England shore. At first, there had been space enough for everyone to co-exist without too much tension, as when the Chadbournes first set up their mill by Mr. Rowle's fish weir. But as more emigrants arrived, the ways that the English and the Native peoples of New England thought about using and occupying land did not mesh as easily. Both, for instance, wanted to be at the falls of rivers, whether for fishing or for the mills the English needed to grind their grain or cut their lumber. The English let their hogs and cattle forage freely in woods and meadows where Native American hunters chased deer—and where those hunters saw little practical difference between beef and venison. Settlers in New England, meanwhile, did not always agree among themselves about what was commons and what was held exclusively. The unwritten custom or private agreement that an emigrant's place in the old country was supportable only in communities where the status of land rarely changed. In the absence of familiar local custom, then, the Puritan emigrants to New England and, much later, the religious Dissenters who founded the Province of South Australia were eager to recreate a sense of permanence and place that had once existed in rural England, hoping as well to nurture morality and religion on a kind of clean slate of a *vacuum domicilium*. Except that neither New England nor South Australia were empty lands.

The question of what that sense of place entailed in a new world would change, however, and this chapter explores how the recordation of land rights reflected and affected that change. While the very first recordation statute, Massachusetts Bay's 1634 order, aimed at confirming place and permanence when it ordered towns to make a list of who lived where and had which rights of ownership or use of commons, the colony's General Court (a combined legislature and court) moved in 1640 to emphasize changes in the status of land. Legislation that year declared that "no morgagye, bargaine, sale, or graunt … of any houses, lands, rents, or other hereditaments, shalbee of force against any other person except the graunter & his heires, unlesse the same bee recorded."[3] It was, the New Englanders quickly discovered, the transfer of land rights even more than establishing a permanent place, that required a public record.

At the same time, the informality of language and slapdash recordation practice suggest that New Englanders were still exploring exactly what rights they were securing or transferring. Mr. Rowle had sold that half mile of river bank "except a Parcell of Ground called by the Name Comphegan" in 1643, but apparently kept crossing over it to fish at the weir. Mr. Rowle eventually memorialized his right to fish there in a follow-up deed three years later, just as Chadbourne made sure he could continue to exploit what was, in effect, a critical portion of a commons: the Great Works River. Neither right was recorded until 1649, two years after Basil Parker began recording deeds in the town book; the deeds between Mr. Rowle and Chadbourne were only the sixth entry. Mr. Rowle and his dependents remained on the banks of the Great Works River for three decades after that first sale to Chadbourne, and two decades after he sold Comphegan for £5 to Thomas Spencer and had swapped "An ould Corne ground" that he had "formerly made vss of & Improved" to Katherine

Treworgy, in exchange for a "Consideration of two bottles of Lyquor to mee In hand." This deed was never recorded, but a posthumous "true copy" was attached to a deed for her son Samuel's sale in 1674 of the 50 acres; the true copy was made in 1676 when Samuel recorded the transactions. His profit was the difference between the two bottles of liquor his mother gave for the 50 acres and the £45 the buyer, a Richard Rich, paid in 1674.[4] There are no other deeds by Mr. Rowle or any other member of his Pennacook band in town records that were later compiled in the York County deed books by the time he summoned the Plantation's leaders to his sickbed in 1675.

Settlers did record seven other land deals with sachems farther up the Maine coast by that time. In one, Scitterygusett, the Sagamore of Casco Bay, said he did "hereby firmely Covenant bargan grant & sell" two tracts of land to Francis Small "To haue & hould & peaceably to possesse & Injoy" including income from "Mineralls fishings fowlings Hawkines [and] huntings." In return, Small promised to pay "one Trading Coate" and a gallon of liquor every year—a rent, that is. Scitterygusett retained an interest in the land for which he would be compensated.[5] Upahannum, also called Jane the Indian, acting for herself, her mother and brother, granted a large tract of land to the Alger brothers "on condition that for tyme to come" the Algers would "suffer Uphannum to plant In Andrew Algers fejld, soe long as Uphannum & her mother Neguasqua doe both live." The Algers were to pay an annual rent of one bushel of corn for the land, an acknowledging Uphannum's continuing connection to the land that the deed declared she had sold.[6] Sagamore John said he did "absolutely give grant & confirm" 20 acres of land to Thomas Watkings "as alsoe for & in consideration for his Travell with & for mee from … Boston to ye Fort of Arania & the great pleasure & good hee did mee there" at that Dutch fur trading post on the Hudson River.[7] While the Englishmen's voices are clearly evident in the wording here, particularly the piling on of terms that describe absolute, unconditional transfer and that promise undisturbed possession, these deeds actually recorded agreements to share land.

The language in some deeds, granting land for "the love and good will" a Native American individual was said to feel for an Englishman, like the annual rent payment, suggest a kind of gift-and-tribute exchange in which a Native America sagamore or sachem acting on behalf of a community makes a gift of access to land and receives a boon in return. This was what exchanges of wampumpeague (the belts of beads made from seashells), liquor, or other goods signified. After the fur trader Simon Willard gave the sachem Tohattowan and her husband, the powwow (spiritual leader) Wompachowet, some clothing, hatchets, hoes, knives, and wampumpeague in exchange for some 36 square miles on the Massachusetts Bay Colony frontier, Tohattowan and Wompachowet declared themselves satisfied and welcomed the English to what they still considered their land.[8] In none of these cases did the Native American grantors have seen themselves as surrendering their own rights to use, pass through, and live on that gift of land. Their recorded deeds and depositions (including those in their own languages) were careful to reserve rights to hunt, fish, or plant on ceded land. Native Americans' words as well as their actions make it clear that they believed they were agreeing to share land. They did not see themselves surrendering rights to use, pass through, and live on that gift of land.

Despite the questions that Mr. Rowle might legitimately have had about what the deeds actually meant or about the price he got—those bottles of liquor—the prospect of war eventually led him to want to declare his own rights to land. As related by one of three witnesses to William Hubbard, the dying Mr. Rowle had "expected some of the English that seized upon his Land should have shown him that Civility, as to have given him a visit in his aged Infirmities and Sickness," as, presumably, good neighbors would do. He was, it seems, concerned that his final wishes be respected for "to be sure at the last," he sent for the leaders of the nearby town of Kittery. When they came, Mr. Rowle said "that though he might as he said to claim all the Plantation for his own where they dwelt," he hoped "they would please to sell or give him a small tract of land" of one or two hundred acres. He asked that the land "might be recorded in the Town Book as a publick Act," so that his children, after his death "might not be turned out, like Vagabonds, as destitute of an Habitation amongst or near the English."[9] Mr. Rowle had, after so many years, come to realize that what he had seen as gift and tribute exchanges that cemented neighborly agreements to co-exist and to define a patchwork of exclusive and shared occupation and use of land were in fact something else. In his view the land was still rightfully his. Rather than pursuing a losing argument against a record, however, Mr. Rowle decided to do exactly what the English had done: record his rights, even if he had to secure them by purchasing his own land. He wanted the permanent place on land that he thought earlier gift and tribute exchanges had secured. Mr. Rowle and the English settlers had, in fact, shared the land for many years pretty much on the terms Mr. Rowle had understood when agreeing to those exchanges. But the looming tensions that would soon erupt into war in 1675 convinced Mr. Rowle that he could no longer count on those agreements. Nor could he count on sharing the land.

That war would temporarily force a community of Massachusett and Wampanoag converts to Christianity off of their land at the falls of the Charles River; the township of Natick that the General Court had granted them. They had for a quarter century "fenced & broaken vp two great Feilds" for the whole community to cultivate cooperatively, as traditional English-style open field arable. This was not the Massachusett and Wampanoag tradition of small, separate plots that women held with exclusive rights of access and to the produce from that land. The Natick converts also had acquired cattle and established in a commons of meadow as pasture, just as their English neighbors had (though those neighbors, unlike some English settlers, had opted for exclusive possession of their cropland and complained that their cattle had been attacked by the Natick people's dogs).[10] But within a generation, the press of English emigration would focus new attention on Natick land, and led town clerk Thomas Waban, son of the first convert, to begin recording land rights. These rights could be as complex: "And now this is the agreement regarding that meadow," one Massachusett language deed, copied into the town record book started. "John Thomas, Senior, remains where he is regarding that meadow, except only that he has lent a little of it to Jonathan Rice. But whenever that becomes open, then that shall be property of Isaac Wuttasukkooppauin." Thomas was then to get from a man named Wunneetomag two acres from the meadow of Samuel Abraim, lying to the south.[11]

In adopting the Puritan settler innovation of recording land rights, Thomas, Rice and Wuttasukkooppauin were trying to confirm a complicated set of relationships among themselves and with the land at a time such rights and relationships were very much in transition. On the one side, the Massachusett, Wampanoag, Nipmuck, and Pennacook faced settlers who (unlike the fishermen and fur traders who had for several decades come for a season to do business and then depart) wanted to plant themselves permanently on land in ways that conflicted with Native communities' customary rights of access, occupation, and use of land. On other side, the English emigrants' own notions about their rights to land were not completely fixed. The language describing specific agreements about land rights was, necessarily, complicated. Thomas did not simply say the meadow was his. He did not sell a portion to Rice, but simply lent a portion of his rights on the meadow to Rice. Those rights were not specified. When Rice no longer wanted to use the meadow, Wuttasukkooppauin was to step in. That part of the meadow, or perhaps, only Thomas' rights to that part of the meadow, were to be his. Thomas was to be compensated for this by access to part of another Englishman's land.

It is worth stressing here that Rice was not seeking permanent possession of Thomas' land, but simply a temporary right use of a portion of it. Thomas' intention was that another member of his Massachusett-speaking community would eventually hold the land, or at least rights to it, going forward, while Thomas would get similar rights on land that belonged to another English settler. All of these complicated arrangements were set forth in a Massachusett language document to reflect what the Massachusett men involved understood about the nature of their old and new land rights were. That the nature of land itself dictated which rights of use and possession applied in Massachusett and Wampanoag law is suggested by deeds recording transactions within those communities as well as with English settlers. Jacob Wahshaman and his wife Wunnattuckquanummow leased a farm to the preacher John Mommanequin for 15 pence a year, but declared in their Massachusett language recorded deed that with the preacher's payments "firmly he owns it and forever."[12] On Cape Cod, Paupmunnuck, acting for himself and a brother, reserved 30 acres out of the large tract he conveyed to the town of Barnstable, for use as cornfields (evidently, by the size of that acreage, for the use over decades of rotating swidden plots, without specifically designating the location of the plots or when they would be cultivated). The deed also made clear that Paupmunnuck would still have the right to continue to hunt and trap anywhere on the tract. The Pennacook sachem Wonalancet reserved a right to continue planting corn on Wichasauke island in the Merrimack River that he sold to an English settler. Wonalancet eventually regained the 60-acre island by convincing the General Court to grant 500 acres of land to the island's owner if he, in turn, would give back the island to Wonalancent.[13] Wadononamin, sagamore of Washucke and Piscataqua, "for the Loue I beare to Englishmen" agreed to "give grant enfeoffee & confirme unto ye sd Edward Hilton Junr all my Lands … only excepting ye vse & improvement of ye one halfe if need be of convenient planting Land for & during my naturall Life."[14]

Permanent, exclusive rights of ownership, however, were not only an English notion: the Wampanoag community of Gay Head, at the western end of Martha's Vineyard island, granted a quarter of its commons to Omppahinnit, declaring in the Massachusett language that "by right this belongs to Ompahinit, him and all his posterity forever," as a 1675 recordation carefully notes.[15] "The Natives are very exact and punctuall in the bounds of their Lands," Rhode Island's founder, Roger Williams, "And I have knowne them make bargaine and sale amongst themselves for a small piece, or quantity of Ground: notwithstanding a sinfull opinion amongst ma[n]y that Christians have right to Heathens Lands."[16] The Massachusett language deed recording David Okes' sale of his old field at Nashsnaamiyasuk to Isaak Wuttuckkamen describes the specific rights of ownership—the fee simple authority of exclusive use and access—when it declared that "therefore, no one shall have the power to do anything within this land."[17] The deed that Sabiah Jootes filed at the Dukes County courthouse to record a land deal with Isaak Takemen declared "Even … my children, they shall not meddle with it."[18] The deal was for fee simple ownership and it was recorded in the Massachusett language to reflect the Native American grantee's view about what he was acquiring. What Massachusett and Wampanoag individuals mainly cared about, as expressed in recorded documents written in their own language, was in what people could do on the land.

English emigrants, too, were focused on recording agreement on who could use land, as much as who owned it. "Wheras it is ordered formrly yt eury man shall haue a crteyne pportion of Swampe," the town of Dedham Selectmen declared in 1636, going forward, the holders of the town's larger town lots could cut three trees and smaller lots two, because some parts of the swamp "have many good Pyne trees groweing & other places fewe or none." The conversion of rights of possession to a right to take trees from what was thenceforth a commons was meant so that "eury man may haue an equall pportion soe neere as may be," the their recorded order continued.[19] A month later, with Samuel Dudly's sale of his 300 acres of meadow and upland to be divided among the four buyers, the Selectmen ordered that part would be kept open as "a somer pasture for milch Cowes," for the use of the town's 30 current households. Those families could let two cows graze there if they paid the four men who bought the meadow and the rest of Dudly's 300 acres the sum of thirteen shillings, four pence.[20] A 1645 grant by the town proprietors of Marshfield said settlers on a neck of land almost completely separated from the rest of the town by a 12-kilometer section of the South River also had the right to let their horses, neat cattle, and sheep loose on the adjacent beach to graze, a right no one else in the town had and a right that forbade anyone from enclosing and claiming ownership on any portion of the beach. This right was upheld in court 185 years later.[21]

The English, in their dealings with one another, like the Native Americans trying to secure the resources they depended upon, were setting rules for behavior when they recorded deeds and other land rights documents. Like those Native Americans, English emigrants wanted to proclaim a permanent place on the land. The Massachusetts Bay General Court recognized this with its 1651 order that recorded deeds say that they memorialized the right "To have and to hold the sajd howse or land, respectively, to the party or grauntee, his Heires and assignes, for euer."[22] There was, that is, no requirement set down the use and access rights or the price detailed in Mr. Rowle's deeds; these were recorded at the discretion and desire of the grantor and grantee. They were recorded in detail because there was no general agreement on what those rights ought to entail.

When Massachusetts Bay Colony Governor John Winthrop challenged purchases of Native land on Aquidneck and Prudence islands by religious dissidents, on grounds that such sales were barred by Massachusetts law, Rhode Island's founder, Roger Williams, replied that 2000 yards of wampumpeage could not have bought the islands. The transaction was not a purchase, he said, for: "The truth is, not a penny was demanded for either, and what was paid was only gratuity."[23] Winthrop should have understood this, for when he first arrived in Massachusetts he brought along counterfeit wampumpeague that he intended to use exactly as the fur traders and fishermen who preceded the Puritans reported the Native peoples of New England had: as a trade item that could serve both as currency and as a memorial of diplomatic agreement over land. It was only when his offer of that counterfeit wampumpeague was not enough to keep Massachusett and Wampanoag men and women away from English towns (perhaps because they could tell that it was fake) that Winthrop began to argue that the land was really empty and free for the taking.[24] He would, for instance, dispute the banished preacher John Wheelwright's right to land he had purchased from Wehanownowit, sagamore of the Piscataqua people, arguing that the land was not Wehanownowit's at the time. The English, instead, had possession "which we took peaceably, built a house vpon it, and so it hath continued in our peaceable possession … which being thus taken and possessd as vacuum domicilium gives vs a sufficient title against all men." Winthrop said no Indian had title to any land, beyond perhaps his or her cornfield. "We conceive that man hath an interest to land 2 wayes: by a naturall right when God gave the earth to the sonnes of men … by vertue whereof any man may make vse of any part of the earth, which another hath not possessed before him …. The other is a Civill right … by attainment of Artes and trades have therby means to improve more lands."[25] Puritan emigrants, Winthrop came to believe, could take that land which "lay open to any that could and would improve it."[26]

The theory that *vacuum domicilium* entitled newcomers to take land in New England was a popular one for the Puritan divines, safely in England, who were promoting emigration. Robert Cushman, the Plymouth colony's agent in London, cited Genesis (though inappropriately) to argue that Massachusett and Wampanoag territory "is spatious and void & there are few and doe but run ouer the grasse, as doe also the Foxes and wild beests." As a result, "it is lawful now to take a land which none useth, and make use of it."[27] Preaching to Lincolnshire Puritans before their departure to Massachusetts Bay (where he would shortly follow) John Cotton reassured them that "Where there is a vacant place, there is liberty for the sonnes of Adam or Noah to come and inhabite, though they neither buy it, nor aske their leaves."[28] Once in Massachusetts, while Salem's Rev. John Higginson would continue to argue that settlers held their land "By a right … whereby God gave the Earth to the Sons of Adam and Noah, to be subdued and replenished," but he would continue to say his congregation also held land "By a right of purchase from the Indians, who were Native Inhabitants, and had possession of the Land before the English came hither."[29] It was "vppon due purchase from the Indians, who were the true proprietours of the land, for we fownd it not a vacuum" that settlers of the New Haven colony settled on the Connecticut shore, that colony's governor, Theophilius Eaton wrote to the governor of New Amsterdam in 1647, challenging the latter's claim to the land.[30] John Eliot, missionary to the Native peoples Massachusetts Bay, arguing for the right of the Praying Indian town of Natick to land that the proprietors of the town of Dedham claimed, said that "Dedham never pcured to themselves the Indians right, who have lived at Natik longer than the oldest man alive can remember" and while "our right we hold … by letters patent from the King's Majesty & by our coming to *vacuum domicilium* where we so find it, but where the Indians have a right, we doe religiously take care that it be lawfully alienated."[31]

There was, wrote Thomas Gage, some two decades after the first English settlers arrived at the Massachusetts Bay Colony, "No question but the just right or title to those Countries appertains to the Natives themselves; who, if they shall willingly and freely invite the English to their protection, what title soever they have in them, no doubt but they may legally transferr it or communicate it to others."[32] Robert Gray, in a sermon urging settlement in America, contended that "there is no intendment to take away from them by force that rightfull inheritaunce which they haue in that Countrey" even though "Some affirme, and it is likely to be true that these Sauages haue no particular proprietis in any part or parcell of that Countrey."[33] The Bay Colony's General Court also recognized that the land was not empty, declaring two decades after the first emigrants' arrival that "what lands any of the Indeans within this jurisdiccon have by possession or improvement, by subdouing of the same, they have just right therevnto, according to that in Geunesis, 1 and 28, chapt 9 : 1, and Psalmes 115: 16"—that is, the Bible verses that say God gave the earth to humans with the command to subdue it and have dominion over all living creatures, that he commanded Noah and his sons to replenish the earth, and that while heaven is God's, he gave the earth to human beings.[34] Even Winthrop would come to recognize this qualification to his *vacuum domicilium*, writing "why may not Christians have liberty to go and dwell among them in their wastelands and woods (leaving them such places as they have manured for their corn) as lawfully as Abraham did among the Sodomites?"[35]

Yet English emigrants could be quite casual about their land. Neither Daniel Howe nor the town of Lynn were entirely sure where his 60 acres were, leading him to petition the General Court to confirm his right to land "because there may be doubt whether it perteyne to the Towne or no."[36] It took John Tompkins 24 years, until 1661, to get around to asking the town of Salem to record his grant of land "if he can tell wher to find it."[37] It was not until 1683 that Thomas Rootes and Henry Kenny settled who owned the land Rootes had received by deed in 1655, without bothering to record it, With no recorded deed, Rootes' brother Josiah felt free to sell the land to Kenny in 1659.[38] Not necessarily sure they had a right to land, or sometimes even where their land was, English emigrants' assertions of their lawful claim had a hollow ring.

Yet the act of recordation, and especially the public nature of the record, was beginning to help narrow the range of agreement over land that the people of Massachusetts would reach by incorporating precise legal terminology. Confirming, in 1735, the right of an English settler to staying a house and some "40 acres more or less," the people of Okokcame village on Marthas Vineyard recorded a deed by which "We give to Elisha Amos a quitclaim deed ('Quiet Claim teet') or to his posterity, or to his kindred; they own this land forever. We, the townspeople of Okokcame, promise that Elisha Amos [shall] have no trouble, regarding this land which we give him."[39] The deed, while recognizing his right to exclusive possession, also makes clear Amos had a right to take trees from the town's woodlands commons. It also gave Amos all of Jonathan Sumana's land, as well as Sumana's rights to allot land as a sachem, and "anything belonging to Jonathan Sumana" because Amos promised to care for him when his relatives would not. A few points implicit here, but worth underlining: Amos had lived in Okokcame for some time without any particularly formal agreement, since he had been able to build a house; he was to have the right community members had to cut wood on their commons; and he was to be recompensed for taking care of member of the community. A still-complex set of an individual's land use and community obligations was set forth in a recorded quit claim deed, in other words.

Promised an empty land only to discover it was already occupied, emigrating from land they had occupied but had not owned, landing on a distant shore where cooperation would be essential for survival, yearning for the permanence of place they had forsaken in leaving England, the Puritans of Massachusetts Bay had moved to set down in writing the terms of their situation on the land. In doing that, one particular definition—simpler and more easily set down in public proclamation—emerged: the idea that you should be able to exclude others from the land you occupied and farmed, from your enclosure, even if actually unfenced and unenclosed. The invisible lines of legalistic language on a page of the town record book defined your land in ways once granted only the lords from whom your independence had been declared in the *Liberties of Massachusetts.* But before too many more decades would pass, there would be new words to redefine the old countries' land, landlords, and their special role in the commercial and financial life of a nation. And the proclamation of those words, eventually to be reinforced by a South Australian legal innovation, would transform the very idea of what land really was.

Notes

1. York County Deed Book 1, folio 1.
2. York County (Maine) Deed Book 1, folios 3, 4, 6, 9, 33, 42; Everett S. Stackpole, *Old Kittery and Her Families* (Lewiston, Maine: Lewiston

Journal, 1903) p. 23. Oliver Godfrey granted the island holding because he "they cannot have Accommodation there," in a recorded deed signed by his father. York Deed Book 1, folio 14.

3. *Records of the Governor and Company of the Massachusetts Bay in New England*, Nathaniel B. Shurtleff, editor (Boston: W. White, Printer to the Commonwealth, 1853) Vol. 1, pp. 306–307. The Plymouth colony had already ordered that "all sales gifts mortgages exchanges leases or other conveyances or leases of houses or land" be "commited to publick record and the fees to be payd," Acts of November 15 1636, in *The Compact with the Charter and Laws of the Colony of New Plymouth*, William Brigham, editor (Boston: Dutton and Wentworth, 1836) p. 43.
4. York County Deed Book 1, folio 6, York County Deed Book 3, folio 10.
5. York County Deed Book 1, folio 83 (1657). Another recorded deed that involved rent, rather than a purchase (in this case of a bushel of corn and a quart of liquor), was from Nanauddenance to John Parker, deed Book 2, folio 13. (1649, recorded 1662).
6. York County Deed Book 2, folio 114 (1672).
7. York county Deed Book 1, folio 32. Other Native American individuals' deeds to English settlers were Thomas Chabinocke to John Wadleigh, 1649, *Ibid.*, folio 126; Rawmegin to Robert Gutch, 1660, Book 2, folio 39; Mogg Hegone to William Phillips, 1669, Ibid, folio 46. Rawmegin's other land sales before Rowle's failed effort to secure land were recorded years later in York County Deed Books III, folio 23 (1660, recorded 1678); IX, 254; X, 252, XI, 139; XX, 86, 87, 88; XXXV, 50 (sale 1639, recorded 1759). Roughly sixty supposed sales by Native Americans in Maine, including several for transactions from the time before Mr. Rowle's failed effort to secure his land were filed in the "Book of Eastern Claims," a logbook of land claims of individuals who fled Maine during King William's War (War of the League of Augsburg) from 1688–1697, M.I. Moore, editor, "Book of the Eastern Claims," *Maine Historical and Genealogical Recorder*, Vols. VI–VIII (1892–1894). These generally have even fewer details than the recorded York County deeds. Emerson Baker, "Trouble to the Eastward: the failure of Anglo-Indian Relations in early Maine," PhD dissertation, 1986, College of William and Mary, p. 127.
8. John Peacock, "Principles and Effects of Puritan Appropriation of Indian Land and Labor," *Ethnohistory*, Vol. 31, No. 1 (Winter, 1984), pp. 39–44; Julie A. Fisher and David J. Silverman, *Ninigret, Sachem of the Niantics and Narrangansetts: Diplomacy, War, and the Balance of Power in Seventeenth-Century New England and Indian Country* (Ithaca: Cornell University Press, 2014), p. 92; Yasu Kawashima, "Legal Origins of the Indian Reservation in Colonial Massachusetts," *The American Journal of Legal History*, Vol. 13, No. 1 (January, 1969), pp. 42–56. For the role of

wampumpeague, see Frank G. Speck, "The Functions of Wampum among the Eastern Algonkian," *American Anthropological Association, Memoirs*, Vol. VI (1919), pp. 3–71. Tohattowan's agreement is recorded in Middlesex County (Mass.) Deed Book 8, folio 105. For the theory of gift and exchange, see Marcel Mauss, *Essai sur le don : Forme et raison de l'échange dans les sociétés archaïques In Sociologie et Anthropologie* (Paris: Presses universitaires de France, 2007 [1923]).

9. William Hubbard, *The Indian Wars in New England*, ed. Samuel Drake (Roxbury, Mass.: Printed for W.E. Woodward, 1865 [first published 1677]) Vol. 2, pp. 263–264.
10. Dedham Town Records, Vol. 4, p. 273; Indian Records, 1602–1705, Vol. 30, p. 261a (1681), Massachusetts Archives, Boston. The Natick converts' farming pattern was like the manorial patter of open field arable and pasture commons that the first settlers in Rowley and Hingham, Massachusetts, adopted. Barry C. Field, 'The Evolution of Property Rights', *Kyklos*, Vol. 42, 1989, pp. 319, 333–4.
11. John Thomas to Jonathan Rice and Isaac Wuttasukkooppauin, Natick town records, loose leaf collection, document 111, translated in Ives Goddard and Katherine Bragdon, *Native Writings in Massachusett* (Philadelphia: American Philosophical Society, 1988) Vol. 1., p. 311.
12. John Mommanequin lease, *Dukes County Registry of Deeds*, Book 1, p. 18, translated in Goddard and Bragdon, Native Writings, p. 107.
13. *Records of the colony of New Plymouth, in New England*, Nathaniel B Shurtleff, editor (Boston: W. White, 1851) Vol. 2, pp. 130–131; Kimball Webster, History of Hudson (Manchester, N.H.: Granite State Publishing, 1913), pp. 36–38.
14. Rockingham County Registry of Deeds, book 3, p. 122.
15. Gay Head community to Omppahinnit, *Dukes County Registry of Deeds*, Book 6, p. 372, translated in Goddard and Bragdon, *Native Writings*, p. 89.
16. Roger Williams, *A Key into the Language of America* (Providence: Rhode Island and Providence Plantations Tercentenary Committee, 1936 [1643]) p. 95.
17. David Okes to Isaak Wuttuckkamen deed, *Dukes County Registry of Deeds*, Book 2, p. 336. Translated in Goddard and Bragdon, Native Writings, p. 93.
18. Sabiah Jootes to Isaak Takemen deed, *Ibid.*, Book 2, p. 338.
19. Selectmen's grants, 31 December 1636 in *The early records of the town of Dedham, Massachusetts*, Don Gleason Hill, editor. (Dedham, Mass: Dedham Transcript, 1892) Vol. 3, p. 26.
20. Selectmen's grants, 28 January 1637, *Ibid.*, p. 27.
21. Briggs Thomas, Complainant, versus The Inhabitants of Marshfield 27 Mass 364 (Supreme Court of Massachusetts, Plymouth, 1830).
22. *Massachusetts Bay Records*, Vol. IV, part 1, p. 39

23. Roger Williams to John Winthrop, 14 June 1638, in *Winthrop Papers* (Boston: Massachusetts Historical Society, 1929) Vol. 4, p. 41. The Massachusetts Bay General Court banned individual purchases of Native land in 1634, *Massachusetts Bay Records*, Vol. 1, p. 112.
24. John Peacock, "Principles and Effects of Puritan Appropriation of Indian Land and Labor," *Ethnohistory*, Vol. 31, No. 1 (Winter, 1984), p. 40.
25. John Winthrop to John Wheelwright (March 1639) *Winthrop Papers*, Vol. 4, p. 102.
26. John Winthrop, *The History of New England*, James Savage, editor, (Boston: Little Brown & Co., 1853) Vol. 1, p. 349.
27. Robert Cushman, "Reasons and Considerations Touching the Lawfulness of Removing out of England into the Parts of America," in *The Journal of the Pilgrims at Plymouth*, George Cheever, editor (New York: John Wiley, 1848) p. 104. Cushman cited Genesis 13:6 11 12 referring to Lot's occupation of land, as well as 34.21, referring to the marriage of Jacob's daughter Dinah and 41.20, referring to cattle grazing.
28. John Cotton, *Gods Promise to his Plantation* (London: John Bellamy, 1630) pp. 4, 5.
29. Testimony of Rev. John Higginson in "The Revolution in New England Justified," in *The Andros Tracts* (New York: Burt Franklin, 1967), Vol. 1, pp. 88–89.
30. Charles J. Hoadley, ed., *Records of the Colony and Plantation of New Haven, From 1638 to 1649* (Hartford: Case, Tiffany and Co., 1857) p. 508.
31. Massachusetts Archives, Vol 30, p. 103A.
32. Thomas Gage, *The English-American his Travail by Sea and Land: Or a New Survey of the West-Indies, containing a Journal of Three thousand and Three hundred Miles within the main Land of America* (London: R. Cotes, 1648) p. 3.
33. Robert Gray, *A Good Speed to Virginia* (London: William Welbie, 1609) n.p.
34. *Massachusetts Bay Records*, Vol. IV, part 1, pp. 102–103.
35. *Winthrop Papers* (Boston: Massachusetts Historical Society, 1929), Vol. II, p. 91.
36. Howe petition in *Note-Book kept by Thomas Lechford, esq., lawyer in Boston, Massachusetts Bay*, Edward Everett Hale, editor, (Cambridge, Mass.: John Wilson & Son, 1885) pp. 247–62.
37. Salem Records, *Essex Institute Historical Collections*, Vol. IX (1869), pp. 51, 64; Vol, XL (1904), p. 118. Tompkins had two grants of five acres each in 1637, in 1661 he was trying to record grants of twenty acres.
38. Rootes v. Kenny (1683), Essex County Quarterly Courts, Records & Files box 1, folder 2, leaf 10.
39. Dukes County Registry of Deeds, Book 7, p. 83.

References

The Compact with the Charter and Laws of the Colony of New Plymouth, William Brigham, editor (Boston: Dutton and Wentworth, 1836).

Dedham (Mass.) Town Records.

Dukes County (Mass.) Registry of Deeds, Books 1, 2, 6.

Massachusetts Archives (Indian Affairs) Vol. 30.

Middlesex County (Mass.) Registry of Deeds, Book 1.0.

Note-Book kept by Thomas Lechford, esq., lawyer in Boston, Massachusetts Bay, Edward Everett Hale, editor, (Cambridge, Mass.: John Wilson & Son, 1885).

Papers of the Winthrop Family (Boston: Massachusetts Historical Society, 1929).

Records of the Governor and Company of the Massachusetts Bay in New England, Nathaniel B. Shurtleff, editor (Boston: W. White, Printer to the Commonwealth, 1853).

Records of the Colony and Plantation of New Haven, From 1638 to 1649 (Hartford: Case, Tiffany and Co., 1857).

Rockingham County (N.H.) Registry of Deeds, Book 3.

Salem Records, *Essex Institute Historical Collections*, Vol. IX (1869), Vol. XL (1904).

York County (Maine) Deed Books 1, 3.

Allen, David Grayson. 1981. *In English Ways: The Movement of Societies and the Transferal of English Local Law and Custom to Massachusetts Bay in the Seventeenth Century.* Chapel Hill: University of North Carolina Press.

Cotton, John. 1630. *Gods Promise to His Plantation.* London: John Bellamy.

Goddard, Ives, and Katherine Bragdon. 1988. *Native Writings in Massachusetts.* Philadelphia: American Philosophical Society.

Gray, Robert. 1609. *A Good Speed to Virginia.* London: William Welbie.

Hubbard, William. 1865. *The Indian Wars in New England*, ed. Samuel Drake. Roxbury: Printed for W.E. Woodward. [first published 1677].

Leavenworth, Peter S. 1999. 'The Best Title That Indians Can Claime': Native Agency and Consent in the Transferal of Penacook-Pawtucket Land in the Seventeenth Century. *The New England Quarterly* 72 (2): 275–300.

Peacock, John. 1984. Principles and Effects of Puritan Appropriation of Indian Land and Labor. *Ethnohistory* 31 (1): 39–44.

Speck, Frank G. 1919. The Functions of Wampum Among the Eastern Algonkian. *American Anthropological Association Memoirs* VI: 3–71.

Waterhouse, Edward. 1936 [1622]. A Declaration of the State of the Colony and a Relation of the Barbarous Massacre. In *The Records of the Virginia Company of London*, ed. Susan M. Kingsbury, vol. III, 557. Washington, DC: Government Printing Office.

Williams, Roger. 1936 [1643]. *A Key into the Language of America*. Providence: Rhode Island and Providence Plantations Tercentenary Committee.
Winslow, Edward. 1865. A Letter Sent from New England to a Friend in These Parts. In *Mourt's Relation, or Journal of the Plantation of Plymouth*. Boston: J.K. Wiggin.
Winthrop, John. 1853. *The History of New England*, ed. James Savage. Boston: Little Brown & Co.

CHAPTER 3

Deeds: Working It Out in Writing, the Evolving Language of Land Deeds

Abstract The language of American recorded deeds grew ever more elaborate in the nineteenth century as the individuals granted access, use, and occupation rights to land sought to pin down exactly what those rights entailed. This urge for precision and tendency of repetitive assertion of rights reflected a broader uncertainty: a basic conflict between a traditional notion (as expressed, e.g. by John Locke) that the human labor that transformed land earned a person rights to that land versus the market ideal that purchase of a particular set of rights, those of fee simple ownership, were fundamental. This conflict of tenure concepts was in the process of resolving to favor fee simple ownership. Economists eschewed the idea that land had an inherent value from its natural attributes to argue that its value was simply as form of capital and its value simply what buyers would pay. Easy recordation and the development of warrants and other securities representing conditional claims to land accelerated this trend.

Keywords Land deeds • Deed recordation • Squatters • Land warrants • Preemption

Lacking either a General Land Office receipt showing that he had paid for a half section of prairie at Round Point (since he had not actually done so) or a court house where he could record any kind of claim to the rich central Illinois land, Henry Simmons simply carved his initials on a "witness

D. Ress, *Deeds, Titles, and Changing Concepts of Land Rights*, https://doi.org/10.1007/978-3-030-64191-7_3

tree" to declare his aim to earn the land by putting up a cabin. He was shot and killed before he could build that home. The next man to try to secure that land, also with initials carved into a tree, had better luck even though he never bothered to erect a cabin. His initials, and his ability to credibly threaten would-be settlers he considered to be claim-jumpers, eventually won a $25 payment from the family that would end up on the land. [1] The form and wording of a public declaration of land rights mattered, for simply to be on the land was, in law, not necessarily to have a right to the wealth it could yield. Moreover, it was that income, more than the right to live on land and use it that was becoming the focus of attention, whether in settler societies such as New England or in the analyses of political economists. "Land is the source or matter from which all wealth is drawn," since the wheat flour in bread and the cloth in a coat embodied land, as Richard Cantillon, one of the first political economists, wrote some 60 years after Mr. Rowle tried to secure his land.[2] At the same time, as seventeenth century New Englanders gradually acquired the habit of recording their right to hold land "for ever" (in the usual language of their documents), William Sheppard's *An Epitome of All the Common and Statute Laws of this Nation* would have reminded them that under the legal system they imported from England that "a man may have a Possession of Lands, to which he hath no Right at all."[3] Still-new theories of law and of political economy undercut the popular feeling that it was what a person did on empty land that won a right to use or occupy that land. Uncertainty reigned—as when, for instance, Alabama's Supreme Court in one year ruled that a squatter could keep his farm even though a group of French emigrants had recorded a formal title to it, while the next year decided that an another French absentee landowner's recorded title barred others from that land.[4] Even in same state, even before the same court and even at about the same time, judges lacked certainty about who ought to be able to exclude whom from land. The idea of what secured a person a place on the land—and, not quite the same issue, a right to income from the land—was unfixed, even in the venue where fixing on answers to such questions was its very purpose.

In response, recorded deeds grew more and more elaborate. Once simple deeds like William Hays' 1806 "informal and usually summary" recordation that "for value received, I bargain and sell unto Arthur Conley my whole right of improvement," would no longer seem adequate to buyers and sellers, even if judges were satisfied that the requirements of law had been met.[5] To some extent, this was because many land transactions involved complex or conditional transfers of rights. In 1820, for instance, the aging Kentucky farmer Peter Ringo, "in consideration of the services which the said Major and Joseph Ringo may render in transacting any business which may be necessary in the premises, doth hereby give, grant and convey, unto the said Major and Joseph Ringo and their heirs, jointly, the whole of the tract or parcel of land on which the said Peter now resides" while the two younger men "thereby, for themselves and their heirs, forever release and quit claim to any other part of the estate of said Peter Ringo" in a deed reserving the older man's right to remain on the land while the younger pair managed it.[6] Here, the deed recorded part of a complicated disposition of one man's estate before his death, while securing him a place to live.

Yet even with simple sales, the piling on of synonyms describing all manner of transfers and of land rights would become automatic, as in the deed from Edmund Phillips and his wife Milley his wife, to George Shepherd. It transferred "all the right, interest and claim, in law or equity, not heretofore conveyed by them, or agreed or covenanted by them, or their ancestor, to be conveyed, which they had, as heirs of Francis M'Dermed, or as heirs of Fanny Wilson, deceased, daughter of the said Francis M'Dermed, to any lot or parcel of ground, situate, lying and being in the town of Lexington, or its vicinity."[7] Unlike the very first recorded deeds in New England, these floods of words were not concerned with resolving differing views of the rights that came with access to and use of land. Instead, they addressed a deeper uncertainty about the real source of rights to a place on the land and to earn a living. This chapter aims to explore that uncertainty and how the words of recorded deeds, as well as the writings of political economists, shaped a clearer consensus about property rights in general and land in particular—a consensus that reduced what had been a complex set of economic and emotional connections to land into an almost purely financial and abstract relationship.

For although many still believed that it was labor on the land that secured a person's place upon it, tension between the ownership of land and cultivation of it that had not been obvious before had emerged and was growing stronger. Arguing for the rights of squatters on Maine's frontier, school teacher Elisha Sylvester reminded the Pejebscot Proprietors of the Casco Bay region of Maine in 1801 that "the celebrated Lock [sic] says, that he who makes any improvement to land in a State of Nature has a better claim to it than any pretended purchaser."[8] Ownership was essentially passive, political economists wrote—the landlord's role was "to reap where they never sowed," as Adam Smith put it.[9] "Land, from its abundance, may be of little value" in any financial sense, declared the South Carolina editor and economist Jacob Cardozo. The American experience showed that "In the first settlement of a country, land is of no exchangeable value; for every one may have as much as he pleases," as Francis Wayland, president of Brown University, noted in his *Elements of Political Economy* (one of the most-read economic texts in America during the first part of the nineteenth century).[10] It was at this point, still work on the land that mattered; buying and selling seemed much less important, at least in theory. It was, however, of increasing interest to those who, like George Washington, George Mason, Benjamin Franklin, and other well-connected colonial Americans seeking ways to invest their funds, saw speculation in land as a way to make money.

Virginia's efforts to sell land in the Kentucky frontier seemed to prove this point. Disappointed by their first efforts to sell frontier land, the new state's officials moved to pique that speculative interest with a new financial instrument—essentially, a primitive derivative security—that allowed a holder to claim land for little or nothing, with full payment later should things work out. Virginia's land warrants were something new in land dealing. Like modern stock options, they established a conditional claim on an asset that required additional payment in order to be exercised and to record ownership of a specific piece of land. By the end of the American Revolution, Virginia issued about 4000 warrants for 1.3 million acres, with one shilling, two pence securing a claim to 1000 unspecified acres, a far smaller sum than outright purchase.[11] The conditional nature of the claim did not bother the speculators who ventured into the game. Patrick Henry gambled £40 on warrants for 10,000 not-yet located acres, even as he opined that £10 for 100 acres of well-located Kentucky land was too little.[12]

The result was chaos—a flood of paper that, in effect, created fictional land. By 1780, John Floyd, an agent for a group of Virginia warrant buyers, warned that warrants already in hand were "sufficient to cover all the vacant land of a tolerable quantity" around the Falls of the Ohio (now Louisville, Kentucky). He reported that an additional 1.6 million acres had not even been recorded, which was the first step of four steps needed to turn a warrants to possession of an actual piece of land.[13] The race to record locations, patents, and eventually deeds of sale of often unmapped and poorly described land routinely meant several claimants battling in court for possession of the same parcels, reported George M. Bibb, a judge on the Kentucky Court of Appeals.[14] Kentucky's legislature complained that the state's people had been "continually alarmed" by speculators, whose claims, backed by copies of recorded patents, grants and deeds served "eventually to cast out naked on the world, numerous well settled and industrious families." It enacted laws declaring that squatting farmers who paid taxes on their land could get clear title if nobody challenged their possession for seven years, and that modest improvements to land along with a promise to pay for the raw land would allow squatters to keep their farms.[15] Recordation, and the validity of recordation, was becoming the focus of a new tension between those who had come to think of land as a financial asset and those who saw only a place where they could live and work.

Despite the confusion caused by Virginia's land warrants in Kentucky, the national government saw these financial instruments as an inexpensive way to reward soldiers who fought in the Ward of 1812, and issued similar warrants for land on the prairies of central Illinois: the Military Tract. Vast stretches of the Military Tract were owned, and recorded as such, but empty.[16] On the Tract, Mercer County had just 26 residents five years after incorporation, while Henry County had 41. In Kentucky, the uncontrolled issue of warrants had created a kind of fictional land. In Illinois, the result was virtual counties—fully elaborated political structures with hardly anyone to govern. Each, however, had a place to register ownership of land, a place to argue about conflicting claims, and men who could collect fees for doing so. What they were missing was people who would actually live on the land. The view out the door of those log-cabin courthouses (windows were luxuries) was of a new kind of land: conceptual land.[17]

The unease that opened the floodgates of legalese was not limited to Kentucky and other frontier states. In a 1795 New York deed that the U.S. Supreme Court described as unusually brief, John J. Van Rensselaer declared that he and his wife Catherine "have granted, bargained, sold, aliened, enfeoffed, assured, released, and confirmed, and by these presents do grant, bargain, sell, alien, enfeoff, assure, release, and confirm, unto the said Daniel Penfield" (repeating this formula one more time later in the document).

> all the right, title, interest, property, claim, and demand, either in possession, reversion, or remainder, of him … together with all and singular the waters, watercourses, and streams of water, profits, advantages, hereditaments, and appurtenances whatsoever thereto appertaining and belonging,

> or which have been considered and used, or now are used and occupied, as part and parcel thereof … and the reversion and reversions, remainder and remainders, rents, issues, services, and profits thereof, and also all leases of and concerning any part or parts of the said granted premises; and also all the estate, right, title, interest, property, possession, claim, and demand of them,

before promising that Penfield, along with his heirs and anyone to whom he might assign his newly acquired interests would forever be able "to have and to hold" and (twice repeated) "in as full and ample a manner as the said John J. Van Rensselaer now hath and enjoyeth the same." This was possible because van Rensselaer "freely and clearly acquitted and discharged of and from all encumbrances and charges, other than leases heretofore given by the said John J. Van Rensselaer and his ancestors, or any of them."[18] This was a transfer of more than 33,658 acres of land in the towns of Claverack and Hudson, New York. But it was more than that, as it also included van Rensselaer's rents from future generations of tenant families on his essentially feudal estate. Landholding—at least from the tenants' view—still might be permanent without necessarily involving ownership, as least in the populous Hudson River valley.

Reassuring the uncertain buyer of his or her rights, particularly those beyond the rights embodied in fee simple ownership, was an important function of wordy recorded land deeds. In a 1785 deed granting state-owned land at Point Judith, Rhode Island, state treasurer Joseph Clarke declared he was "fully satisfied, contented, and paid" and would therefore "exonerate, acquit, and discharge" the two buyers "their heirs, executors, administrators, and assigns forever" of any further demand for money and did "fully, freely, and absolutely give, grant, bargain, sell, alien, enfeoff, convey, and confirm unto" them, their heirs and assigns forever, three lots of upland and three lots of marsh

> together with all and singular the ways, waters, rights, libertys, privileges, improvements, hereditaments, and appurtenances whatsoever unto the hereby granted premises belonging or in anywise appertaining, and all the estate, right, title, interest, inheritance, possession property, claim, and demand … to have and to hold the said granted and bargained premises, with all the hereditaments, appurtenances, privileges, and commodities to the same belonging, unto them … and to their heirs and assigns forever, to their only proper use, benefit, and behoof forever, as a good and perfect Estate of Inheritance in fee simple, free and clear of all incumbrances,

whatsoever, which might in any measure or degree obstruct or make void this present deed.

Although not spelled out specifically in the deed, the repeated declaration of all rights involving the land included the right to gather seaweed from an adjacent portion of shoreline commons, the Rhode Island Supreme Court would rule, nearly a century later.[19]

Public documentation of land rights became increasingly more important than the Lockean notion that "As much land as a man tills, plants, improves, cultivates, and can use the product of, so much is his property." Recordation also overrode Locke's point that to claim more than what "any one can make use of to any advantage of life before it spoils … is more than his share, and belongs to others."[20] Lacking a record of his father's right to some 96 acres of orchards, cornfields, and woods called Cheney's Delight on Maryland's Conococheague Manor, Jeremiah Cheney found himself at risk of being thrown off the land, 54 years after his father started farming there. The reason was because Thomas Ringgold recorded his purchase of the land from his grandfather's other heirs a few years earlier. Ringgold's grandfather, despite living 200 miles from Conococheague Manor, had secured a patent to the land some 16 years after the elder Cheney started farming there but had not recorded it. Justice John Buchanan, of the Maryland Court of Appeals, in a decision reflecting Locke's limit on how much land a person could properly claim, split the difference. The judge ruled that Cheney could keep his enclosed fields, but Ringgold could have the rest.[21] Long occupation was no longer enough to secure land. So, even though the neighbors who had helped him build his cabin and raise his barn recognized his right to his farm, Braxton Parrish was not sure of his right to his land after 16 years of living there. That was why, after those many years, he went ahead and paid the fees to record his ownership of his Franklin County, Illinois, farm.[22] After a jury of Indiana farmers in 1821 ruled that their neighbor, a Mr. West, should remain on the farm he carved out of the Harrison County wilderness, the only way the judge could think of to validate their opinion was to seize upon the technicality that the man who recorded a deed to the land had not been formally traced through four transactions to the original federal patent. The state supreme court overturned that ruling.[23] A Lockean right was not the most secure way to hold land, as Samuel Turner discovered when he came back to his Illinois Military Tract land from a trading trip to St. Louis to find another man settled in his cabin. Rather than simply throw the intruder out, Turner gamely set out to raise another cabin and clear a farm in the Buena Vista Township, only to lose it in 1834 to a man who had recorded a Land Office patent for the land. Turner moved one more time to a farm "which he had to pay for no less than three times before finally securing a perfect title" and recording the deed that did so.[24]

Recordation made possible the conversion of the shared title to the Iowa Half Breed Tract, a reservation set aside by treaty for the children of Sac and Mesquakie women and white fur traders, trappers, and soldiers. The treaty granted "Indian title" to some 119,000 acres of land between the Mississippi and Des Moines rivers "for the use of the half-breeds belonging to the Sock and Fox nations."[25] Although the treaty did not name individuals, and although longstanding American law barred individuals from buying or selling Native American land, a considerable trade in Half Breed Tract land emerged once a new court house began recording deeds. Recordation here established, first, an assertion that the seller had a claim to a specific piece of land (though its location and boundaries were typically undescribed in any meaningful way); second, that he or she was able to sell that land, despite the terms of the treaty and third, that the buyer, upon recording the deed now had the right to do whatever he or she pleased, including selling it. A circle of lawyers practising in the county court house where the deeds were recorded, along with the county judge (who also served on the territorial supreme court), acquired some of these deeds and bid for control of the whole Tract. (The lawyers acted both for themselves and for treaty rights holders and individuals who had purchased land, all of whom were disputed any other person's rights to land.) The judge, first in the county court and then later reviewing his own decision in his role as a justice of the territorial supreme court, confirmed the courthouse cabel's ownership of the Half Breed Tract.[26] Their coup was overturned by the U.S. Supreme Court in 1850 decision that simply confirmed the rights of a settler who had recorded a deed to a quarter section of land that the lawyers claimed they owned. In so doing, the Supreme Court effectively nullified the supposed shared title of the treaty rights holders.[27]

A somewhat different game of deeds—in this case, involving sales by the same man of the same land to two different buyers—led Wisconsin's Supreme Court to follow an emerging judicial rule that when a deed fell short of what a statute said it should contain in order to be recorded, it did not represent a valid title even if recorded. The case, decided in 1866, resolved a dispute over some 600 town lots in the port city of Superior. Because the first deed had no certificate that the notary public who acknowledged it was in fact a notary, it did not meet the standard set by Wisconsin's land records statute. That in turn meant the deed did not do what a properly recorded deed was supposed to do: provide general notice to the public of the status of the land. That, then, meant that the second deed, recording a sale a year later, memorialized a valid transfer and that grantee, and his subsequent grantees, had title to the land.[28] In Kansas, Isaac Johnnycake's sale of the portion of a former Native American reservation he lived on was deemed valid, even though he did not in fact have formal title to it. This was because of the formula used on his 1867 deed. It said Johnnycake "grants, bargains, sells, aliens, releases, quitclaims and conveys" to Kate L. Simpson "together with all the improvements, ways, easements, rights, privileges and appurtenances to the same belonging or in anywise appertaining, and all remainders, reversions, rents, issues and profits thereof, and all the estate, right, title, interest, claim and demand, either at law or in equity, or otherwise howsoever of the said (Johnnycake) in, to, or out of said premises."[29] That long series of verbs and descriptions of what he was transferring aimed at fending off any challenge to the deal. And it succeeded.

This nineteenth century concern with following the rules and insistence on precision in details marked a change from earlier, more casual judicial attitudes. Where once, judges accepted state laws that held no transfer of land was valid if not recorded, they were inclined to brush off arguments about the form of the documents recorded, as when Virginia's Supreme Court rejected a bid to invalidate an improperly indented recorded deed.[30] Legislation to simplify and lessen the amount of paperwork "for example by enacting that two words shall of the effect of twenty formerly used" aimed to facilitate transfer and reduce dispute.[31] Beginning in 1817, Massachusetts's Supreme Judicial Court held that when a would-be buyer of land checks the seller's deeds and liens in the Recorder of Deeds office and finds a valid conveyance, there was no need to look beyond that. New York courts, however, ruled that the record of a prior deed, even if recorded till after the second deed, meant that a would-be buyer needed to look further into the status of land.[32] In 1885, New York City acted to make searches simpler by compiling an index of every block of land that noted then-current status; a technique adopted by private abstracting firms and title insurers.[33] Validation of land title did not normally go beyond such an abstract of deeds records, and validation largely devolved on the insurance companies that stepped in to sell policies to indemnify buyers and their creditors in the event a title was, in the end, invalid. This was initially a business in cities and their suburbs "since rural tenures are long-term, the title changes are infrequent, and most titles, even though originally defective, have been perfected by adverse possession." Abstracts, however, eventually spread to the countryside, too.[34]

Even so, the formulae of deeds remained elaborate. When John Lisle sold his land in Howard County, Missouri in 1867 to Charles and Anna Bukley, he did so by a deed that "does hereby grant, bargain, sell alien, release and convey unto them … To have and to hold said lands, with all and singular, the appurtenances thereto attached and belonging unto them … free from the claim of him, the said John E. Lisle, and also free from the claim or claims of all and every person whatsoever."[35] In 1882, Peter Berger "granted, bargained, sold, aliened, enfeoffed, released, and confirmed and by these presents doth grant, bargain, sell, alien, enfeoff, release, and confirm unto" his niece Sally Serfass a life interest in 50 acres. In return, she promised to "bind myself, my heirs, executors and administrators and every of them firmly by these presents, which are to be considered on my part as a deed of covenants, to find good house-room and sleeping and lodging apartments for the convenience of the said Peter Berger during his life and to find good and sufficient board, lodging, meat, drink, clothing and nursing, medical attendance and all other necessaries for him during his life and a decent burial for him when he leaves this world of sorrows."[36] While deeds could record arrangements other than outright ownership, even when they did address fee simple possession, they piled on words: the man who sold Emma Root her house in Jacksonville, Florida, in the 1880s wrote a deed to "grant, bargain, sell, alien, convey and confirm" the house to her and her heirs and any people to whom she might later assign ownership, "to have and to hold the aforesaid bargained premises together with all and singular the rights, members, tenements, hereditaments and appurtenances to the same … to her and their own sole and proper use, benefit and behoof in fee simple," using the archaic term to describe use for a person's own benefit.[37]

The English philosopher Jeremy Bentham captured the still-evolving sense of rights to land when he concluding that the value of any piece of land could vary with "the certainty or uncertainty of its coming into possession: and the nearness or remoteness of the time at which, if at all, it is to come into possession."[38] The economist and university president Francis Wayland wrote that because "The title to land can be more definitely secured than that of any other property" since "The legal instruments, by which it is secured to individuals, are a matter of public record." The point was that "ownership" of it can always be ascertained and passed on to posterity.[39] Wayland was still, in his rather old-fashioned New England way, concerned with the ability for a family to stay on land through generations, while Bentham's point about coming into possession of land included the possibility of transfer to others. The ability to sell land, once there was some way to validate the landholders' legal right to do so, including by recordation, would become more and more important in economics texts. This was why the American economist Willard Phillips believed that it was only through the ability to buy and sell real estate that land became valuable. Goods that are free for the taking have no value, so there was no reason to hold them, he wrote. Moreover, the distinction between landholders (his term) and owners of capital goods vanished once "lands are alienable at will," he added.[40] Land, in the English political economist Nassau Senior's view, was merely an instrument of capital. Its value simply reflected "the number of those instruments compared with the number and wealth of the persons able and willing to hire them."[41] Like a government bond or a corporate share certificate, to hold land was to hold a financial asset. Recordation made the similarity that much clearer.

The crusty retired colonel turned free trade campaigner Robert Torrens fretted, with Senior, about what to do about displaced rural laborers. Like Senior, he also concluded that land and capital goods—and the income that came from owning either—were fungible. The problem, he would eventually decide, is that "the supply of labour has such a tendency to exceed the demand for it that the labouring classes" who are then "commonly reduced to a degree of distress and temptation … and of morals there is no conceivable remedy except in a system of colonization sufficiently extensive to relieve the mother country from superfluous numbers."[42] Yet with colonization "The most rapid accumulations of capital might be made" and "commerce and the consequent division of employment, between the old and the new country … would give the wealth and resources of England the capability of an almost infinite increase."[43]

Torrens would shortly put action to words, investing in a scheme to promote a settlement in New Zealand's Bay of Islands. After the failure of that effort, frustrated that his fierce advocacy of such liberal causes as repeal of the Corn Laws and Catholic Emancipation in his journals *The Traveler* and *The Globe* kept him from securing a seat in Parliament, Torrens sought land and a government position in the Swan River Colony in Western Australia.[44] It was at this time that Robert Gouger, who had left his father's merchant business and was also considering a move to Swan River, brought together Torrens and Sir Robert Wilmot-Horton, a member of Parliament fresh from service as under-secretary for war and the colonies, in a failed effort to resolve a dispute within the National Colonisation Society over land policy. Gouger had been working with Edward Gibbon Wakefield while the latter was imprisoned for abducting a 15-year-old heiress, on what was to become his famous *Letter from Sydney* pamphlet proposing a system of concentrated settlement with controlled land sales at a high price.[45] What if, Wakefield had written, the United States General Land Office asked £9 per acre, instead of its 9 shilling ($1.25) price for western lands. "There would be no buyers, you think," he answered, "of course not, until the people had increased so as to render land, already appropriated, worth more than nine pounds per acre."[46] The £9 per acre price he proposed "would gradually cause appropriated land to yield a rent … This would be an enormous benefit conferred upon the American landlords," he argued.[47] Rent, in turn, could be used to finance immigration, and immigrants' desire for land would keep rents on the rise.[48] It would be a self-funded process of growing national wealth, Wakefield argued.

Torrens was skeptical at first, focused, as were so many other political economists, on a vision of vast, uncultivated stretches of fertile land in America. But he would be convinced by the already evident difficulties of the Swan River Colony, where land was free for the taking, and by Gouger and Wakefield's framing of concentration as a way of focusing capital and labor on the production of goods. Torrens' focus on manufacturing as the source of Britain's future prosperity meant he was indifferent to the implication that land would no longer be the pre-eminent factor of production (as the earliest political economists had believed) but merely a kind of capital, subject to a price determined by a market and in balance with a demand from immigration. A year later, with Torrens as its chairman, the colonization society submitted its first proposal (in the form of a pamphlet) to the Colonial Secretary for settlement of South Australia.[49] Three years later, Parliament approved a colony, with immigration financed by the controlled sale of land in concentrated settlements.[50] Now, it was to be the certainty that a sale was valid, more than the certainty of permanent possession, that would come to matter most.

Notes

1. N. Matson, Reminiscences of Bureau County (Princeton, Ill.: Illinois Republican, 1872) pp. 50–54.
2. Richard Cantillon, *Essai sur la Nature du Commerce en General*, Chantal Saucier, translator, (Auburn, Ala.: Von Mises Institute, 2010 [1730]) p. 21.
3. G.E. Aylmer, "The Meaning and Definition of 'Property' in Seventeenth-Century England," *Past & Present*, No. 86 (1990), p. 93.
4. James Childress against Francis McGehee; 1 Minor 131 (Alabama Supreme Court, 1823); White v. Saint Guirons, 1 Minor 331 (1824).
5. Deed conveying improvements to Arthur Conley cited in Chiles v. Conley's Heirs, 2 Dana 21 (Kentucky Court of Appeals, 1820).
6. Deed of lease to Major and Joseph Ringo, cited in Young v Ringo, 17 Ky 30 (Kentucky Court of Appeals, 1824).
7. Cited in Phillips v Green 21 Ky 355 (Kentucky Court of Appeals, 1827).
8. Alan Taylor, *Liberty Men and Great Proprietors: The Revolutionary Settlement on the Maine Frontier, 1760–1820*, Chapel Hill, 1990, p. 101.
9. Adam Smith, *An Inquiry Into The Nature and Causes of The Wealth of Nations* (New York: Bantam, 2003 [1776]) p. 70 (I xi, 5).
10. Jacob N. Cardozo, *Notes on Political Economy*, (Charleston, S.C.: A.E. Miller, 1826) pp. 31, 38; Francis Wayland, *Elements of Political Economy* (New York: Leavitt, Lord & Co., 1837) p. 382.
11. Isaac Harrell, "Some Neglected Aspects of the Revolution in Virginia," *William and Mary Quarterly*, 2nd series, Vol. 5, No. 3 (July, 1925) p. 159.
12. *Ibid*., p. 164.
13. John Floyd to William Preston, May 5, 1780, cited in C.H. Laub, "Revolutionary Virginia and the Crown Lands (1775–1783)," *William and Mary Quarterly*, 2nd Series, Vol. 11, No. 4, (October., 1931), p. 311.
14. Paul Gates, "Tenants of the Log Cabin," *Mississippi Valley Historical Review*, Vol. 49, No. 1 (June 1962) p. 4.
15. *Acts of Kentucky, 17th General Assembly*, Frankfort, 1809, p. 85; *Acts of Kentucky, 20th General Assembly*, Frankfort, 1812, p. 117.
16. For military bounty land warrants and their impact, see Theodore L. Carlson's classic, *The Illinois Military Tract, A Study of Land Occupation, Utilization and Tenure* (Urbana, Ill.: University of Illinois, 1953). Speculator John Tillson acquired more than 450 square miles on the Military Tract by 1833 and James Stapp had 57 square miles, but the 1840 Census would show only fourteen ex-soldiers living on the Tract. Carlson, *The Illinois Military Tract*, table 9, p. 58; *Census of Pensioners of Revolutionary and Military Service*, Washington, 1841, pp. 186–88.
17. U.S. Census of 1830.

18. Cited in Van Rensselaer v. Kearney, 52 U.S. 297 (Supreme Court of the United States, 1851) at 299.
19. Knowles v. Knowles, 12 R.I. 400 (Supreme Court of Rhode Island, 1879).
20. John Locke, *Two Treatises of Government,* ed. Thomas Hollis (London: A. Millar et al., 1764), p. 220. (Book 2, chapter 5, paragraph 31).
21. Cheney v Ringgold et al. Lessee, 2 Harris & J 87 (Maryland Court of Appeals, 1807).
22. Braxton Parrish, "Pioneer Life in Egypt," *Golden Era*, No. 36, 4 September 1874. The Illinois Public Domain Land Tract Sales Book, vol. 110, p. 73 shows Parrish's first purchase of land, 37.87 acres in the "southwest-southwest" lot of Section 19, Township 6-South, Range 4-East of the Third Meridien on Oct. 10 1836. He bought 120 acres in 1850, Book 105, p. 43 and 75 acres in 1853, Book 112, pp. 16, 49.
23. Doe, on demise of Wood v. West, 1 Blackf. 133 (Indiana Supreme Court, 1821).
24. W.R. Brink (editor), *Combined History of Schuyler and Brown Counties, Illinois*, (Philadelphia: W.R. Brink & Co., 1882) p. 60.
25. Treaty with the Sauk and Foxes (August 4, 1824) 7 Statutes at Large, 229.
26. David Ress, *The Half Breed Tracts in Early National America: Changing Concepts of Land and Place* (New York: Palgrave Macmillan, 2019) pp. 63–76.
27. Webster v Reid 52 U.S. 437 (U.S. Supreme Court, 1850).
28. Ely v. Wilcox, 20 Wis. 523 (Wisconsin Supreme Court, 1866).
29. Bruce v. Luke, 9 Kan. 201 (Supreme Court of Kansas, 1872).
30. Currie v Donald 2 Va. 58 (Virginia Supreme Court, 1795).
31. Dorr Viele, "The Problem of Land Titles," *Political Science Quarterly*, Vol. 44, No. 3 (September, 1929), p. 423.
32. Connecticut v. Bradish, 14 Mass. 296 (Supreme Judicial Court of Massachusetts, 1817); Trull v. Bigelow, 16 Mass. 406 (Supreme Judicial Court of Massachusetts, 1820).
33. Jackson, ex dem. Merrick v. Post, 15 Wend. 588 (New York Supreme Court of Judicature 1836).
34. Viele, "The Problem of Land Titles," p. 430; Edward H. Cushman, "Torrens Titles and Title Insurance," *University of Pennsylvania Law Review and American Law Register*, Vol. 85, No. 6 (April, 1937) pp. 589–612.
35. Cited in Major v. Bukley, 51 Mo. 227 (Supreme Court of Missouri, 1873).
36. Cited in Dreisbach v Serfass, 126 Pa. 32 (Supreme Court of Pennsylvania, 1889).
37. Cited in Harwood v. Root, 20 Fla. 940 (Supreme Court of Florida, 1884).
38. Jeremy Bentham, *An Introduction to the Principles of Morals and Legislation*, (Oxford: Clarendon, 1907 [1823]) p. 32.

39. Francis Wayland, *Elements of Political Economy*, (New York: Leavitt, Lord & Co., 1837) pp. 399–400.
40. Willard Phillips, *A Manual of Political Economy with Particular Reference to the Institutions, Resources and Condition of the United States*, (Boston: Hilliard, Gray, 1828) pp. 28, 118.
41. Nassau Senior *Political Economy* (London: Richard Griffin & Co. 1855) 3rd edition, p. 139.
42. Robert Torrens, *An Essay on the Production of Wealth* (London: Longman, Green, 1821) p. 252.
43. *Ibid.*, p. 259.
44. Torrens, Robert, "*Dictionary of National Biography*," Sidney Lee, editor, (London: Smith Elder & Co., 1909) Vol. XIX, pp. 993–994; Torrens, Robert (1780–1864), "Australian Dictionary of Biography," National Centre of Biography, Australian National University, http://adb.anu.edu.au/biography/torrens-robert-2740/text3873, first published 1967. Lionel Robbins, *Robert Torrens and the Evolution of Classical Economics* (New York: Macmillan, 1958) p. 146.
45. Gouger, Robert (1802–1846), "*Australian Dictionary of Biography*," National Centre of Biography, Australian National University, http://adb.anu.edu.au/biography/gouger-robert-2109/text2581, [1966].
46. Edward Wakefield, *A Letter from Sydney, the Principal Town of Australasia*, London, 1829, pp. 170–171.
47. *Ibid.*, p. 177.
48. *Ibid.*, p. 178.
49. National Colonisation Society, *Proposal to His Majesty's Government for founding a colony on the southern coast of Australia* (London, 1831).
50. An Act to empower His Majesty to erect South Australia into a British Province or Provinces and to provide for the Colonisation and Government thereof (4 & 5 Will. IV c. 95).

References

Acts of Kentucky, 17th General Assembly, [1809].

Acts of Kentucky, 20th General Assembly, [1812].

American State Papers, Public Lands.

An Act to empower His Majesty to erect South Australia into a British Province or Provinces and to provide for the Colonisation and Government thereof (4 & 5 Will. IV c. 95).

Australian Dictionary of Biography.

Connecticut v. Bradish, 14 Mass. 296 (Supreme Judicial Court of Massachusetts, 1817).

Currie v Donald 2 Va. 58 (Virginia Supreme Court, 1795).

Doe, on demise of Wood v. West, 1 Blackf. 133 (Indiana Supreme Court, 1821).
Dreisbach v Serfass, 126 Pa. 32 (Supreme Court of Pennsylvania, 1889).
Ely v. Wilcox, 20 Wis. 523 (Wisconsin Supreme Court, 1866).
Harwood v. Root, 20 Fla. 940 (Supreme Court of Florida, 1884).
Jackson, ex dem. Merrick v. Post, 15 Wend. 588 (New York Supreme Court of Judicature 1836).
Major v. Bukley, 51 Mo. 227 (Supreme Court of Missouri, 1873).
National Colonisation Society, *Proposal to His Majesty's Government for Founding a Colony on the Southern Coast of Australia* (London, 1831).
Trull v. Bigelow, 16 Mass. 406 (Supreme Judicial Court of Massachusetts, 1820).
VanRensselaer v. Clark, 17 Wend. 25 (New York Supreme Court of Judicature, 1837).
Bentham, Jeremy. 1907 [1823]. *An Introduction to the Principles of Morals and Legislation*. Oxford: Clarendon.
Birkbeck, Morris. 1818a. *Notes on a Journey in America from the Coast of Virginia to the Territory of Illinois*. London: Severs & Co.
———. 1818b. *Letters from Illinois*. London: Taylor and Hessey.
Brink, W.R., ed. 1882. *Combined History of Schuyler and Brown Counties, Illinois*. Philadelphia: W.R. Brink & Co.
Cantillon, Richard. 2010 [1730]. *Essai sur la Nature du Commerce en General*. Trans. Chantal Saucier. Auburn: Von Mises Institute.
Cardozo, Jacob N. 1826. *Notes on Political Economy*. Charleston: A.E. Miller.
Carlson, Theodore L. 1953. *The Illinois Military Tract, A Study of Land Occupation, Utilization and Tenure*. Urbana: University of Illinois.
Cushman, Edward H. 1937. Torrens Titles and Title Insurance. *University of Pennsylvania Law Review and American Law Register* 85 (6): 589–612.
Gates, Paul. 1962. Tenants of the Log Cabin. *Mississippi Valley Historical Review* 49 (1): 3–31.
Harrell, Isaac. 1925. Some Neglected Aspects of the Revolution in Virginia. *William and Mary Quarterly*, 2nd series 5 (3): 159–170.
Laub, C.H. 1931. Revolutionary Virginia and the Crown Lands (1775–1783). *William and Mary Quarterly*, 2nd Series 11 (4): 304–314.
Locke, John. 1764. *Two Treatises of Government*. London: A. Millar et al.
Parrish, Braxton. 1874. Pioneer Life in Egypt. *Golden Era* 36.
Robbins, Lionel. 1958. *Robert Torrens and the Evolution of Classical Economics*. New York: Macmillan.
Senior, Nassau. 1855. *Political Economy*. 3rd ed. London: Richard Griffin & Co.
Smith, Adam. 2003 [1776]. *An Inquiry Into The Nature and Causes of The Wealth of Nations*. New York: Bantam.
Torrens, Robert. 1821. *An Essay on the Production of Wealth*. London: Longman, Green.

Viele, Dorr. 1929. The Problem of Land Titles. *Political Science Quarterly* 44 (3): 421–434.

Wakefield, Edward. 1829. *A Letter from Sydney, the Principal Town of Australasia*. London: J. Cross.

Wayland, Francis. 1837. *Elements of Political Economy*. New York: Leavitt, Lord & Co.

Wilkinson, W.S. 1904. A Pioneer Settlement in Madison County. *Annals of Iowa* VI (6): 447–454.

Wood, William. 1865 [1763]. *New England's Prospect*. Boston: The Prince Society.

CHAPTER 4

South Australia: Registration and the Market for Land

Abstract Founded on an ideal of well-ordered settlement of empty land, early South Australia had neither. The answer, proposed by Robert Richard Torrens, the son of one of the colony's most active promoters, was a system of registering titles to land through which the state certified fee simple ownership. The idea of ownership was basic here, for subsidized emigration of a labor force as well as public works were to be financed by sales of Crown Land—land, that is, that had belonged to Aboriginal peoples whose use and access rights were supposed to be protected but in fact were not.

Keywords Land title • Title registration • Land ownership • Ordered settlement • South Australia

The town was supposed to be a neat grid of 1000 one-acre homesteads, with 38 lots carefully set aside for public squares. But "Every man had built his house on the spot which whim or chance pointed out or where material was easiest got and the consequence was that a collection of as primitive looking wigwams as can be well imagined soon lined the banks" of Adelaide's River Torrens.[1] In the trash-filled empty lots that dotted the town, left that way for "mere technical points, affecting title," South Australia's provincial treasurer found "grounds sufficient to urge our

D. Ress, *Deeds, Titles, and Changing Concepts of Land Rights*, https://doi.org/10.1007/978-3-030-64191-7_4

Legislatures to prompt action in eradicating a system of law which, like a noxious fungus, swells by absorbing into itself vital elements essential to the production of wealth."[2] For Robert Richard Torrens, son of one of the colony's founding fathers, the chaos of early Adelaide was a reminder of the "misery and ruin which fell upon a relation and dear friend" by the "grievous injury and injustice inflicted under the English Law of Real Property." [3] He thought he had an answer, though. It was a notion that arose from his somewhat swashbuckling days as the provincial Collector of Customs, when a system of registering owners of ships would be one of the tools he used in what was apparently a distinctively aggressive enforcement of commercial law. As Collector he had sparked a small international incident after setting off in a whaleboat after a French vessel, which he had heard was illegally transporting 2000 sheep to Western Australia (a trip reserved for British or colonial vessels). The ship eventually returned to Holdfast Bay after a comic-opera three-day chase in which the province's customs steamer kept missing the French vessel as it tacked back and forth across Gulf St. Vincent. In the end, since the French ship had not loaded enough food for the crew, it was forced to return to Holdfast Bay after the angry (mostly Australian) crew overpowered its captain and supercargo. Torrens' initial, over-hasty move to seize the ship, acting on tip before it had actually loaded the sheep owned by an influential grazier, nearly led to its release, but later evidence of its intention to violate the Navigation Act led to its eventual seizure.[4] Torrens was nothing if not bold.

As indeed was the very idea of South Australia. The colony was founded on a theory about land value and capital; specifically, that setting a high base price for land would ensure self-supporting development. "The colonization of South Australia by industrious and virtuous settlers," wrote John Stephens, an active promoter of the colony,

> is a necessary preliminary to the displacement of the lawless squatters, the abandoned sailors, the runaway convicts, the pirates, the worse-than-savages that now infest the coasts and islands along that extensive portion of New Holland and perpetrate against the defenceless natives crimes at which humanity revolts.[5]

For the aim, after all, as expressed by the House of Commons itself in authorizing the colony, was "to promote among [the Aborigines] the spread of civilization and the peaceful and voluntary reception of the Christian religion," Stephens noted.[6] That purported aim for the new province of South Australia was much like that expressed on the seal of the

Massachusetts Bay Colony, with its image of an Indian saying "Come over and help us" as he held an arrow pointed down in a gesture of peace. Like Massachusetts Bay, South Australia was not the first British settlement on a new continent. Like the Bay Colony, too, South Australia was intended from the start to be a permanent haven for religious dissenters, as opposed to the plantation agriculture, fishing station and fur trading posts that were the first colonies in North America or the Australian prison colonies.

"My great object," said George Fife Angas, founder of the South Australian Company,

> was, in the first instance, to provide a place of refuge for pious Dissenters of Great Britain … Then, in the second place, to provide a place where the children of pious farmers might have farms on which to settle and provide bread for their families.[7]

In practical terms, wrote Torrens's father, the political economist Robert Torrens, the colony's future depended on the "rapid reproduction of capital when applied to fertile soil" by an "industrious population bestowed upon the colonial lands."[8] It was the tension between that vision of ordered British settlement (with Aborigines in their separate mission stations) and the sprawl that so bothered the younger Torrens that would seem to demand public proclamation of the status of any particular piece of land. That desire for order, undermined by an urge to spread out and freely exploit South Australia's resources, and the consensus about land-holding that emerged, with the help of the land title registration system Torrens created, are the subjects of this chapter.

To see this, it will be helpful to revisit Newgate Prison and the former King's Messenger, Edward Gibbon Wakefield, serving his term for abduction of his child bride and thinking about the vexed questions of rent and profit, land, and capital goods. In his *Letter from Sydney*, as he pretended to be an Australian instead of the jailbird he in fact was, Wakefield argued that it was careful management of the geography—specifically, a well-ordered concentration of population—that would make a new colony prosperous. When land was free for the taking, as it was for the tens of thousands who squatted on public land in North America (or, indeed, in New South Wales, for those squatter pastoralists who ran their sheep on the grasslands west of the Great Dividing Ridge), there could be no rent to keep the price of foodstuffs high (and what we would now call the real wages of labor low). Low wages meant more profit for the capitalist;

profits that could be used for further investment and more production of goods in the future. "I had fancied that … that CONCENTRATION would produce what never did and never can exist without it: CIVILIZATION," he wrote.[9]

Describing an American west he had never seen, Wakefield argued that "in all new countries" where "the most fertile land can be obtained for nothing, the superior fertility of land is worth nothing."[10] The real value of land, as distinct from the exchange price that Willard Phillips emphasized, was not merely a return for the bounty of Nature but also how close it was to towns and their markets. In New South Wales, he argued, "the most fertile land will not, unless near a town, yield any rent at all,"[11] Wakefield wrote. He insisted that an attribute of specific, real pieces of land—where they were located—might generate value, even in a new country.

Elaborating on this theme of the high value of land, he imagined asking Robinson Crusoe what would happen if an earthquake destroyed his land. "Robinson, pointing to the inclosure, said 'We have plenty left food for a year, seed, tools and goats, capital, sir, I think you called them.'" But what, Wakefield imagines asking, "is the use of capital with no more than this little bit of land?"[12] Land makes the difference, for if the earthquake had not destroyed his land, Crusoe's capital and Friday's labor would have assured both an adequate livelihood, Wakefield continued.[13] New land offers a way past this destructive confrontation, but not if managed in the American way, Wakefield argues:

> When a people cultivate land of very great natural fertility and without limit as to space so that the people may increase without resorting to inferior soils they have no inducement to employ their industry in the most skilful way … America is the example…[14]

Breaking step with other liberal political economists of the day, including his ally in promoting South Australia, Col. Torrens (Robert Richard Torrens' father), Wakefield put land at the center of theory again, though not in the same way that Cantillon and his followers had. Theirs had been, in a sense, a political theory; that a class of people, the class defined by their ownership of land, were the motor that drove and gave direction to a nation's commerce. Later writers, including Adam Smith and the leading English economist of the day, David Ricardo, saw land as merely one factor of production, with fertility determining yield, both in terms of produce and income. Wakefield's view was geographic: that the organization of society in space, that where land was and how much was exploited were the critical questions. The right amount of land brought into production would ensure the best use of capital and most prosperous situation for labor; both Crusoe and Friday, that is, would benefit.

Col. Torrens, like the other new political economists wrestled with the challenges of Poor Law reform, including the displacement of tenants, farm laborers, and smallholders from the English countryside. Linked to this was what could seem an explosive (or perhaps cancerous) growth of urban industry and slums. For Torrens and many of his contemporaries, these trends demanded a focus on capital and how it was deployed. Land had come to seem to them to be merely a kind of capital, or, alternatively, a blank upon which capital was deployed; the production of goods from the resources contained in land was in this view a simple function of capital. (In his Crusoe parable, Wakefield said other English political economists were "a new sect" who "have set up a new God, which is called capital, and which they worship devoutly.")[15] The more capital, the more production, and the better, in Torrens's analysis. Torrens saw the return from capital, profit, as the determinant of the total goods production of a community, and thus of the prosperity (the average prosperity) of its people. Wakefield, on the other hand, saw the price of land as a regulator that set a community's mix of land, labor, and capital.

Torrens' and Wakefield's differences in emphasis came down to the role of capital. Torrens favored importing as much capital and as many capitalists as possible. Wakefield called for striking a balanced mix of labor and capital to assure maximum production from carefully delimited land on the other. As a result, they disagreed about the price at which land was to be sold. Wakefield had thought £2 an acre would be appropriate (though far lower than the £9 figure he had proposed in the *Letter from Sydney*). The South Australia Act set a 12 shilling minimum and Torrens proposed a £1 minimum price, the compromise from the 17 shilling 6 pence figure the other commissioners favored and Wakefield's £2 figure.[16]

Both Torrens and Wakefield, however, shared a conviction that a dictated price for land could act as a kind of market signal to bring the labor and capital necessary to realize the full potential of the land. The difference in the prices of land each proposed also reflected a difference of opinion about the role of labor. Wakefield, on the one hand, thought a high price for land would mean landless laborers could command high wages when they first landed in South Australia and so earn the wherewithal to eventually buy land for themselves. Torrens, on the other hand, felt a lower price would encourage buyers eager to put their capital into land, hiring labor at a relatively modest wage to quickly ensure the colony's contribution to the Empire. Both reflected the then-standard view of English political economists, led by Ricardo though already coming under fire in the United States, that land in its natural state had an inherent value, reflected in the rent it yielded.

As land was not over-easily bought and sold in early nineteenth century England, it was to this stream of rental income that English political economists turned when thinking about land as a factor of production. But "Where lands are alienable and as in the United States change possessors as often almost as ships," the price of land, like the price of a ship, was "predicated upon the net income," as Torrens's and Wakefield's contemporary from New England, the American economist Willard Phillips, wrote, in an analogy likening land to the largest single capital good any of the three of them would have known.[17] Land, that is, was essentially capital rather than a distinguishable factor of production with its own distinctive characteristics and management imperatives. The implications of this way of thinking about land, a perception that on Phillips' part was facilitated by the adoption of Massachusetts-style deed recordation across the United States, would be profound. The rapid spread of the land-as-capital concept was about to accelerate, thanks to South Australians' concerns about their place on the province's land.

To assure the colony's viability—for after all, as historian Douglas Pike put it, "In its beginnings South Australia was a land job"—the authorizing legislation required the commission sell £35,000 worth of land orders and raise £20,000 as a guarantee fund.[18] The commission hit the land sales figure by selling some 58,995 acres (none of them actually identified) at 12 shillings an acre in 1835. In 1836, once the contingent was met an evidently less frantic commission sold 1680 acres at 12 shilling each and 240 acres for £1 each.[19]

Complicating sales of land, at whatever price, the Colonial Office reminded Torrens that unsurveyed land could not be apportioned since "numerous Tribes of People, whose Proprietary Title to the Soil, we have not the slightest ground for disputing" might be living there.[20] In reply, Torrens wrote that it was "an established fact, that the unlocated tribes have not yet arrived at that stage of social improvement, in which a proprietary right to the soil exists," although his Colonization Commission would shortly promise to respect Aboriginal rights to land "wherever such right may be found to exist."[21] That right, which seemed non-existent to Torrens, sitting in London, would seem much clearer to those officials who, like Governor of South Australia George Grey, had actually encountered Aborigines. "Landed property does not belong to a tribe, or to several families, but to a single male," Grey wrote, adding "every native knows those of his own land, and can point out the various objects which mark his boundary."[22] Matthew Moorhouse, the colony's Protector of Aborigines, reported Aboriginal "families owning and holding certain districts of land which pass from father to sons ... with as much regularity or propriety as in our own country."[23]

Yet "If the land is indeed their own," a letter from "An Old Settler" published in the *South Australian Register*, argued, "the Colonists of South Australia have no title to their land, for a 'voluntary surrender' of it has never been made."[24] Although Governor George Gawler directed the Protector of Aborigines to step in and select land for the "use & benefit" of the colony's native peoples ahead of any other claimants as surveys were completed, this ended up being a single spot, a missionary station at Moorundie. This was a place too dry for farming, and instead of reserving land for Aborigines, the government ordered the area magistrate to make a "periodical distribution of flour to the natives ... They are to assemble every other full moon for the purpose of receiving these presents."[25]

Pressure for land mounted. The clamor for country land from the holders of the 1835 land orders, the sale of which had financed the colony in the first place, grew ever louder in those first years. So did the contending demand for land from later arrivals, stuck in their huts and tents in Adelaide. "It is a very common thing amongst the settlers ... to make strangers believe that there is not an inch of room unoccupied anywhere," wrote Francis Dutton, the discoverer of the copper deposit at Kapunda, in South Australia's Barossa Valley. "Somehow or other, however, more and more country is notwithstanding continually being made available as the settlers require an extension of room for the increase of their flocks and herds."[26] The government, in response, pushed its survey department for a much more extensive cadastral mapping than first planned. It had set aside Wakefield's concentration model. Impatient colonists began dealing in land and land orders among themselves, in a speculative frenzy. After the first distribution of town lots to holders of land orders (the orders that had been sold for 12 shillings an acre in 1835) the commission auctioned off remaining Adelaide parcels for £2 to £20 an acre. "I have known many instances of parties who then purchased their land at that price dispose of it within the ensuing three years at prices varying from 200 to 2000 per acre," James Bennett reported. In Adelaide and the nearby hills "It was at one time a favourite scheme to lay out a section of land as a township and dispose of the land in minute portions to labourers, mechanics &c. … in many cases the site is only discernible by a board containing its name or the name of some of the streets with the pegs which mark the boundaries of the lots," Bennett added.[27]

Unlike early Massachusetts, where settlers organized through a charter from the General Court to form a town, would set out for unapportioned land, clear fields, and apportion the land to the families that intended to use it, the South Australians waited for a survey to divide land into town and suburban lots for eventual sale. In addition, the government commissioned special surveys of large tracts of country land. The idea was that great landlords were to settle tenants there, in the traditional English fashion. In addition, the South Australia Act of 1834 not only gave the Colonization Commissioners authority to sell land, but also "for the letting of the common of pasturage of unsold portions," to allow large-scale raising of sheep and cattle. Ownership, that is, was not the only way South Australians would define their place on the land.[28] But the certainty that mapping and staking lots was supposed to bring did not come easily. "The Survey department was reduced to the deputy surveyor general, one draughtsman and one assistant surveyor; its instruments to a great extent unserviceable and its office with scarcely any maps of the country and totally without system records or regulations," Dutton remembered.[29] "When I arrived," Governor Gawler reported in January 1839, "I found the public offices with scarcely a pretension of system—everyone did what he wanted, and got on as he could."[30]

The same seemed to be the case outside government offices, as well. "Land of every description in town and country obtained a fictitious value and changed hands over and over again and always at a profit but without making the land productive," Dutton observed. "People living on the Park Lands, as we were, only did so on sufferance," the settler and teamster John Chambers recalled, adding: "Extra liberty was given to me because I had a good deal to do with the Government. We did all the Government carrying work, and moved surveying parties wherever they required."[31] The lack of good information about who had what rights to which land made matters all the wilder.

The colonial government was eager to sell land, especially when Colonel Torrens floated the idea that the Land and Emigration Fund could be tapped for government purposes as well as to finance emigrants. It was so eager, in fact, that it would simply issue receipts stating that it had been paid for a parcel of land. The land would be identified only by a rough drawing in the margin of the document and a reference number for the parcel that made sense only by inspecting the district map in the offices of the Surveyor General.[32] These documents, kept by the landholder and not deposited anywhere for public inspection, did not feature the elaborate piling on of words to describe the act of transfer or the nature of the rights transfers or the grantors' warranty that they had the right to convey land of American recorded deeds. For one lot in Walkerville, bought and resold three times before ending up in the lands of two laborers who sold it for £20 to a newly landed clerk from England, only the laborers' oral recitation of the trail of transactions and a tattered receipt validated with the several previous, illiterate owners' marks in lieu of signatures would serve as title to the land.[33] In one suburb, buyers of its quarter-acre lots received a spadeful of soil in lieu of a paper title, in an apparent recreation of an old English ritual of a change of leasehold tenancy.[34]

Perhaps not surprisingly then, it was almost as soon as the first colonists landed, eyeing the land they had been promised and that Aborigines occupied, that the notion arose that they ought to be able to set down their own land rights on paper and in a way that could be inspected. The first Public Land Commissioner, James Hurtle Fisher, proposed a registration system for land titles, as well as births, marriages, deaths, and wills, but the sweeping power to intrude in colonists' private affairs proved too much for colonial officers, with Advocate General Charles Mann deeming the idea preposterous while the colony's chief judge, Sir John Jeffcott, "openly laughed" at the idea.[35]

But confusion over who had what rights to which land continued, and just a few years later, the colony's new chief judge, Charles Cooper, worried about a flood of lawsuits to settle uncertain titles to land, suggested a public office to receive records memorializing land deals, much as the early New England town clerks had done. The idea was to include only "such information as necessary to prevent fraud without disclosing more" rather than the more intrusive matters that Fisher had proposed that landowners file with him.[36] The Legislative Council enacted Cooper's idea in 1841, "to prevent secret and fraudulent conveyances (of land) and to provide means whereby the title to real property may be more certainly known" and required filing a record of conveyances and liens against land with a new official, the Registrar-General.[37] The explorer Charles Sturt assumed that office, after his failed bid to be named the colony's governor. In 1852, after Sturt's successor as Register won the post of Colonial Secretary, the controversial Collector of Customs, Robert Richard Torrens, son of the old colonel, stepped into the role of Registrar-General.

From the time his friend and relative lost land back in England, the younger Torrens had been convinced that the complexities of English land law, and the secrecy that surrounded conveyancing, badly needed reform. He thought, rather as the American economist Phillips had, that analogy to dealings in the largest capital good of all might offer an answer. "My official employment in the Customs Service during seventeen years made me conversant with the Law of Shipping … I was enabled to perceive that my object might be attained by applying to land the principles which regulate the transfer of shipping property," he wrote.[38] Shipping registries, that is, confirmed title. So would the acts of the registrar in certifying a change of ownership, rather as American states' departments of motor vehicles do now when issuing a certificate of title to a car or truck, while keeping its own record of title. This type of document records ownership, any debts secured by the vehicle and data that could affect the value of the vehicle upon resale, such as mileage or whether it had been in a serious wreck.

Torrens's proposal would have government officials step into the role that Massachusetts law had left for private parties to sort out in court, when there were questions about the status of land. Recordation allowed people to see for themselves by allowing (and eventually requiring) the filing of some sort of memorial of a conveyance or lien, as the South Australia Registration of Deeds Act did. But in his new post as Registrar-General, it seemed to Torrens that South Australia land law remained beholden to an unfair English tradition. The complications of investigation, the possibility of unrecorded claims, such as those of a spouse or heir or purchaser or creditor with a privately held deed predating the recordation act, could still cast a shadow over title to land. "[T]he South Australian freeman had to hold his homestead by a sort of covert imposture that would not bear exposure to daylight," as one newspaper letter-writer complained as well as a growing popular conviction that it was time for the people of a new Australian society—a new democracy—to make up their own minds about the laws they needed. "The prevailing feeling with a very great majority is ultra-democratic," the *Adelaide Times* noted, with some dismay.[39]

For South Australia had just won the power of self-government, with the new South Australia Constitution Act gaining Royal Assent in June

1856. It called for elections in March 1857. There was to be universal manhood suffrage to a 37 member General Assembly. Property-qualified voters would also elect an 18-member Legislative Council replacing the old appointed body. Torrens decided to stand. He based his bid for office on a call for title registration on the shipping registry model, arguing that a democratic Australia needed to shed trappings of English land law that were designed to protect an aristocracy.[40] The idea spread. "The yeomen farmers of Yatala greeted its exposition with the like enthusiasm at a meeting in Salisbury" that May, Torrens recalled.[41] Intrigued, South Australia's largest landowner, George Fife Angas, asked Ulrich Hubbe, a lawyer who had emigrated from Hamburg only to fail on his lease-holding in the Barossa Valley and turn to teaching languages, to draft legislation for title registration, modeled on Hamburg's land law.[42]

Torrens introduced his registration bill in June, but after a first reading in the General Assembly, it stalled—oddly, because there was little opposition to it, except for those lawyers whose main business was conveyancing. Even large landowners accepted that the reform would have little impact on their own capacity to fend off any challenge to their land titles.[43] The delay, perhaps, was due to Torrens' ambition to be premier. Once he achieved that office in September, his bill began moving again, passing its third reading in the Assembly by a vote of nineteen to seven and, after a sixty-foot-long petition signed by 2700 was delivered to the Legislative Council, by that body at the end of January.[44] Under the act, a certificate of the Registrar-General and two commissioners gave indefeasible title to land. The Land Titles Office held the certificate, with a copy for the landowner. Any subsequent mortgages or other liens would be noted on the certificate. A sale would generate a new certificate; the old one would be invalidated. Title to land, in short, was assured by the provincial government, and not by the efforts of an attorney poring through private records or the eyes of an interested individual, paging through grantor indices and deed books in a county courthouse or Recorder of Deeds office.

Torrens, who would resign his Assembly seat to take charge of the Land Titles Office, saw title registration as more than a mere paperwork reform. "In Australia the great mass of the people are, or confidently look to become, landed proprietors," he wrote in a tract explaining the new title registration act. "In Australia, therefore, thorough law reform is essentially the people's question."[45] Torrens contended that the conveyancing lawyers' argument that land was somehow essentially different than property, like ships, that could be moved, reflected the distinctive pattern of land rights in England, "held by a comparatively small number of proprietors"...

> handed down in the same family from father to son for generations, so that transfers are rare, and when they do occur are for amounts so considerable that the costs of conveyancing, great though they may be, amounting on the average to two and a half percent on the purchase-money.[46]

The complexities of English land law, Torrens continued, could be "clearly traced to the subtle devices resorted to in feudal times in order to evade the tyrannical exactions of arbitrary power."[47] Those complexities were maintained by the "high conservative feeling of the landowners of England tending to maintain the feudal principle of inalienability in contradistinction to the modern principle of convertability," an anachronism that inhibited progress.[48] For:

> In England in ninety nine cases out of one hundred the property is in a highly improved state when possession is taken and its value far exceeds the sum expended in improvement by the existing occupier. In the colonies all this is reversed; the improvements are in nine cases out of ten effected with capital of the party in possession ... and the land itself is of little value compared with the sum invested on it in improvements Hence a rule of law sufficiently grievous in the old country inflicts an amount of wrong positively outrageous when applied to countries still in the course of settlement.[49]

Settlement, that is, which displaced an indigenous people. The risk to settlers and potential for injustice became clear, Torrens continued, when in the days before his title registration act took effect the Supreme Court of South Australia invalidated the sale of some 131 acres in Adelaide. The sale, by the Indian Insolvency Court as it settled debts of a bankrupt speculator, netted £1600 from settlers who then built homes, a bishop's palace, and schoolhouse, altogether worth somewhere between £13,200 and £14,500. The Australian court ruled that the land belonged to that bankrupt's heir-at-law on the grounds that the land titles issued by the Indian court were invalid. "Here the English law, as administered by the Supreme Court, in restoring to the rightful heir his patrimony ... would bestow upon him therewith the patrimony of persons innocent of any fraudulent intention,"[50] Torrens wrote. Title registration, by validating a sale and wiping clear any preexisting potential claims, was like the recordation of deeds granted to Massachusetts Bay colonists for the supposed love and good will of the Native American grantor, a way of reassuring settlers who considered themselves innocent of any intention of taking land of the Aborigines they had promised to, as they put it, civilize. "To think that these beings are really of one blood with us," the South Australian novelist Matilda Evans (writing as Maud Jeanne Franc) had one of her conscience-struck settlers comment, before adding: "Does it not seem strange? They have souls, and yet how near they seem to approach the lower order of animals."[51]

Often, disputes over title to land would not even end up in court, Torrens wrote. For "the parties frequently surrender without litigation, aware that the expenses of a chancery suit would swallow up the entire property. Three such cases are at this moment pending in this colony within the knowledge of the writer," he added.[52] In this concern for lost capital is an echo of his father's overriding concern to bring investment funds to the new colony. In the younger Torrens's argument that "In Australia, therefore 'thorough law reform' is essentially 'the people's question,'" there is an echo of the colony's founders, whose view was perhaps best summed up by Robert Gouger when he wrote "I put the disposal of land first and the principles of government second … a good government cannot make a new colony prosperous where the means by which public land becomes private property are badly arranged."[53]

Registration provided a sense of security, particularly important in an Australia where "the great mass of the people are or confidently look to become landed proprietors," but where their right to land seemed clouded, whether by the disappointed promise of easy access or a lingering awareness that there were others, the Aborigines, who were there first.[54] Frontier settlers fortified their homesteads, for fear their Aboriginal neighbors take back their rights to land, and pangs of conscience could still bother many in Adelaide or in Britain. Validation of rights to land by the government itself was reassuring. After all, "Colonisation is undertaken for the advantage of the emigrating people, and the aboriginal races stand in the way of the immigrants" one London editor commented, "The great progress of Victoria and South Australia has mainly to be attributed to the ease with which the colonists dispersed over the fine tracts of land which these colonies contain."[55]

But easy dispersion was not Wakefield's idea for South Australia. He wanted concentrated settlement, and for all the tensions within the Colonization over his insistence on a £2 per acre price, the colony's founders did not want to see the kind of rapid spread of squatters and warrant holders experienced in places like the Illinois Military Tract or trans-Mississippi River territories like Iowa, Kansas or Nebraska. The Waste Lands Act of 1842 allowed Australian colonial governors to prohibit the sale of Crown land located up to five miles from a designated town "on the Ground that they will not in his Judgment derive any increased Value from their Vicinity to any such Town." Set a limit on how much land beyond such suburban districts might be sold at any auction and held that no land could be sold for less than £1 per acre.[56] In 1846, Parliament authorized grazing leases of up to 14 years on Crown lands while setting stiff fines for squatting.[57] The 1857 act, reiterating the first Waste Lands Act's provision for a minimum £1 per acre price, empowered the governor of South Australia to set a higher floor price for land outside of town sites.[58]

Easier commerce, however, was the aim of Torrens and the voters who, despite his oddities of character, sent him to the legislature on the strength of a campaign about a bureaucratic process. In South Australia, statutory law was clear about the nature of tenure: Crown land could be sold and was then held in fee simple or could be used for grazing under a long-term lease. But after an initial allotment by agents of the Crown, whether by the first allocations of land to the first settlers who had paid their money, on speculation, to the Colonization Commission, or the later public auctions of town lots, suburban land or land in the country districts through which Aborigines still lived, came complications. "Mercantile men repeatedly ask," Torrens would write:

> —'How comes it that I can, and do constantly transfer property to the extent of many thousands in the funds and in shipping with safety, at a trifling cost and with great rapidity and ease; yet when desire to purchase a rood of land not worth £50 I am at once involved in uncertainty, put to considerable expense and trouble, and delayed for months before the paltry transaction can be completed.'[59]

It would be such easier dealing in land, even more than a promised security of tenure, that would be the most remarked-upon result of Torrens' system. In just two years, some 5776 transactions had gone through the registrar's office, so that something like one in three householders had registered land transfers or financings, Frederick Sinnett reported. "In addition to the saving of some ninety per cent in the cost conveyancing" the new system had benefited colonists "chiefly by restoring to its intrinsic value a large amount of property depreciated or unmarketable," he added.[60] Henry Gawler, examiner of titles, would still later report that "the Torrens' system is a complete success, land in fact being as easily and as securely dealt with as stock in the funds."[61] And a century later, in an essay examining the system and urging its adoption in the United States, the editors of *The Yale Law Journal* reviewing Torrens' system declared: "land today is principally a mercantile commodity, and saleability a primary incident of its ownership."[62] Torrens had found a way past the strictures of English law that discouraged the breaking up and sale of a landed families' holdings, the inalienability that he saw as a feudal hangover unsuitable for a democratic society of people on the move toward bettering their situations. Permanence of place, either on the land or within a social and political structure, didn't matter as much as it once did.

Torrens was far from alone in feeling this. For South Australians, yearning for Victorian British respectability, yet not completely comfortable amidst the strange flora and fauna of their new homes, the complexities and traditions of English tenure made little sense. Torrens's land title system seemed practical. It reflected the colonists' belief from the first days of settlement that buying land was a real option, even for former laborers and tenant farmers. Torrens's title certificates made it simple for Adolph Dorney needed to describe his rights on five lots be bought from Richard Andrews in 1859 was for his certificate of title to say he was "seised of an estate in fee simple," after that same description on a certificate had reassured Andrews of his rights when he bought the lots five months earlier. So too for George Fintine and Mary Bell when the first flipped his Adelaide lot to her just ten months after he bought in in 1860 and the wheelwright Johann Kloke when he sold his 198 acres outside Adelaide to Gottlieb Hoffman two weeks after Kloke acquired the land. Dealing in land was far easier than in England; easier, as far as the paperwork went, than with Massachusetts-style deed recordation.[63]

Still, South Australians nevertheless felt something for their strange new land beyond the rights that purchase or lease allowed. There was something more involved in land reform than the economics of investment that had worried Torrens when he considered those trash-filled vacant lots in Adelaide. He would make this point in response to those English political economists, including W. Stanley Jevons, recently returned to England from his post as an assayer in Sydney, who argued that conveyancing was a trivial burden on land transactions, already reflected in the price of land. Jevons pioneered the new mathematical economics that saw the decisions individuals made as functions of the marginal costs and benefits of buying or selling one more item or making one further investment; any of which were expressed in the price of it did not matter what good or service. Expressed in pounds, shillings, and pence, land could seem like any other good: ultimately, the hundred acres of South Australia that cost you £200 was the same thing as the new Steinway piano that sold for about the same price. Torrens, on the other hand, believed that "All the world over" …

> there are conditions arising out of the ownership of land which tend to enhance its price comparatively with that of other descriptions of property. For example, the feeling of exhilaration which most men experience when treading on their own land. The social status it confers, and the agreeable occupation it affords. [64]

Land was still sometimes something different than a piece of capital equipment, such as a railroad locomotive, or the railway debentures that represented a claim on the income that locomotive could generate, even as the paperwork system Torrens had implemented made the buying and selling of land all the simpler. Yet all the complex attachments people felt toward land remained, even as the basic legal connection they could forge was more and more limited to simple ownership. Making it easier to alienate land, through title registration, did not alienate people from feeling those connections to a place, though over time the new system, like deed recordation, would tend to signal that only those who owned any particular patch of land were entitled to such sentiments of attachment to it. There remained a basic tension here: land was a commodity, subject to what economists like Jevons modeled as rational economic decisions, yet land was also something special, even after its status could be summarized on the front page of a South Australian certificate of title. How these someone dissonant perceptions played out as Torrens' system spread is the subject of the next chapter.

Notes

1. Michael Llewellyn-Smith, *Behind the Scenes: The politics of planning Adelaide* (Adelaide: University of Adelaide Press, 2012) p. 28; James Bennett, *Historical and Descriptive Account of South Australia* (London: Smith, Elder & Co., 1843) p. 15.
2. Robert Richard Torrens, *The South Australian system of conveyancing by registration* (Adelaide: Register and Observer, 1859) p. 26.
3. *Ibid.*, p. v.
4. Douglas J. Whalan, "Torrens, Sir Robert Richard (1814–1884)," *Australian Dictionary of Biography*, National Centre of Biography, Australian National University, http://adb.anu.edu.au/biography/torrens-sir-robert-richard-4739/text7869, published first in hardcopy 1976; James Hunter, History Trust of South Australia, 'Ville de Bordeaux', SA History Hub, History Trust of South Australia, http://sahistoryhub.com.au/things/ville-de-bordeaux, accessed 6 October 2019.
5. John Stephens, *The History of the Rise and Progress of the new British Province of South Australia* (London: Smith, Elder & Co., 1839 (2nd edition)) p. 69.
6. *Ibid.*
7. George Fife Angas to Edwin Hodder (no date) in Edwin Hodder, *George Fife Angas, Father and Founder of South Australia* (London: Hodder and Stoughton, 1891) p. 239.
8. Robert Torrens, *Plan of an Association in Aid of the Irish Poor Law* (London: Longman, Orme, 1838) p. 14.
9. Edward Wakefield (under the pseudonym Robert Gouger), *A Letter from Sydney, the Principal Town of Australasia* (London: J. Cross, 1829) p. 98.
10. *Ibid*, p. 175.
11. *Ibid.*, p. 176.
12. Edward Gibbon Wakefield, *England and America, a Comparison of the Social and Political State of Both Nations* (London: Richard Bentley, 1833) Vol. 1, pp. 113–114.
13. *Ibid.*, p. 124.
14. *Ibid.*, pp. 124–125.
15. *Ibid.*, p. 114.
16. Wakefield to Gouger, 25 May 1835, in Hodder, *George Fife Angas*, p. 164; Book of Regulations for Disposing of Land in South Australia, 19 June 1835, C.O. 386/142.
17. Willard Phillips, *Manual of Political Economy* (Boston: Hilliard, Gray, Little & Wilkins, 1828) p. 118.
18. *Outline of a plan of a proposed colony to be founded on the south coast of Australia, with an account of the soil, climate, rivers, etc.* (London, 1834);

Douglas Pike, "Introduction of the Real Property Act in South Australia," *Adelaide Law Review*, Vol. 1, No. 2 (1961) p. 169.

19. Douglas Pike, Paradise of Dissent: South Australia 1829–1857 (Melbourne: Melbourne University Press, 1967) p. 179.
20. George Grey (Undersecretary of War and Colonies) to Torrens, 15 Dec. 1835, CO 13/3, PRO.
21. Torrens to Grey, Dec. 1835, CO 13/3, PRO; "First Annual Report of the Colonization Commissioners for South Australia," 14 June 1836, British Parliamentary Papers: Colonies: Australia, 4:480.
22. George Grey, *Journals of Two Expeditions of Discovery in North-west and Western Australia, During the Years 1837, 38 and 39* (London: T. & W, Boone, 1841) Vol. 2, p. 232.
23. Moorhouse to Colonial Secretary, 27 July 1840, SA Despatches, CO 13/16, PRO.
24. *South Australian Register*, 1 August 1840.
25. Gawler to Lord John Russell (Secretary of State for War and Colonies), 1 August 1840, CO 13/16; Grey to Edward Eyre, 1841, cited in Robert Foster and Amanda Nettlebeck, *Out of the Silence: The History and Memory of South Australia's Frontier Wars* (Mile End, S.A.: Wakefield Press, 2018) p. 37.
26. Francis Dutton, *South Australia and its Mines, with an Historical Sketch of the Colony* (London: T. &W. Boone, 1846) p. 93.
27. J.F. Bennett, *Historical and Descriptive Account of South Australia* (London: Smith, Elder & Co., 1843) pp. 17, 132.
28. An Act to empower His Majesty to erect South Australia into a British Province or Provinces and to provide for the Colonization and Government thereof (4 & 5 Will. IV c. 95).
29. Dutton, *South Australia*, p. 22.
30. Gawler to Glenelg, 23 Jan 1839, SA Miscellaneous Correspondence, CO 13/14, PRO, London.
31. Dutton, *South Australia*, p. 39; John Chambers, Letter, *Observer*, 14 January 1888, p. 13.
32. Pike, "Introduction of the Real Property Act," p. 173.
33. Poulden to Cooper, 2 May 1839, cited in Pike, "Introduction of the Real Property Act," p. 174.
34. *The Advertiser* (Adelaide), 19 July 1938.
35. *South Australian Register*, 22 September 1838.
36. Cooper to Gawler, 17 August 1840, cited in Pike, "The Introduction of the Real Property Act," p. 176.
37. Registration of Deeds Act, 5 Vic. No. 8.

38. Robert Richard Torrens, *The South Australian System of Conveyancing by Registration of Title* (Adelaide: Register and Observer Printing Offices, 1859) p. vi. Simplification and a desire to standardize go far to explain the introduction and rapid spread of Torrens's system in Australia, historians there have argued. See, for example, R. Stein and M. Stone, *Torrens Title* (Sydney: Butterworths,1991); Douglas Whalan, *The Torrens System in Australia* (Sydney: Law Book Company, 1982); R, Stein, 'Sir Robert Richard Torrens and the Introduction of the Torrens System', *Journal of the Royal Australian Historical Society*, Vol. 67 (1981), pp, 119–131; Douglas Pike, "Introduction of the Real Property Act in South Australia," *Adelaide Law Review*, Vol. 1, No. 2 (1961), pp. 169–189; Theodore B. F. Ruoff, *An Englishman Looks at the Torrens System: Being Some Provocative Essays on the Operation of the System after One Hundred Years* (Sydney: Law Book Company of Australia, 1957); Angas Parsons and A.L. Campbell, "The South Australian Centenary of Legislation," *Journal of Comparative Legislation and International Law*, Vol. 18, No. 1 (1936), pp. 21–39.
39. *South Australian Register* 1 July 1857; *Adelaide Times*, 16 July 1851.
40. *South Australian Register*, 2 February 1857; Torrens, *The South Australian System*, pp.vi–vii.
41. Torrens, *The South Australian System*, p. vii.
42. Ulrich Hubbe, *The Voice of Reason and History Brought to Bear Against the Present Absurd and Expensive Method of Transferring and Encumbering Immovable Property* (Adelaide: 1857), cited in Antonio Esposito, "Ulrich Hubbe's Role in the Creation of the 'Torrens System' of Land Registration in South Australia." *Adelaide Law Review* Vol. 24 (2003) p. 284.
43. Pike, "Introduction of the Real Property Act," p. 179.
44. South Australia Parliamentary Debates, 1857–1858, pp. 760 (19 January 1858,), 773, 778–779 (26 January 1858). The petition is reported in the South Australian Register, 6 January 1858.
45. Torrens, *The South Australian System*, pp.vi–vii.
46. *Ibid.*, p. 6.
47. *Ibid.*, p. 42
48. *Ibid.*, p. 7.
49. *Ibid.*, p. 25.
50. *Ibid.*, p.26.
51. Matilda Evans (Maud Jeanne Franc), *Golden Gifts* (London: Sampson, Low, Marston & Co., 1911 [1867]) p. 61.
52. Torrens, The *South Australian System*, p. 26.
53. Robert Gouger, *South Australia in 1837 in a Series of Letters, with a Postscript from 1838* (London: Harvey and Darton, 1838) p. Viii.

54. Torrens, *The South Australian System*, p. 7.
55. Nicolas K. Grguric, Fortified Homesteads: The Architecture of Fear in Frontier South Australia and the Northern Territory, ca 1847–1885. PhD dissertation, Flinders University; P.L. Simmonds, "The Ethnological Collection at the International Exhibition," *Journal of the Society for Arts*, Vol. 22, no. 1134 (14 August 1875) p. 821.
56. 5&4 Victoria, Ch 36, sections VII, VIII, and XI.
57. 9&10 Victoria, Ch 104, sections I and IV.
58. 18&19 Victoria ch 56, sections 2, 8, and 9.
59. Torrens, *The South Australian System*, pp. 9–10.
60. Frederick Sinnett, *An Account of the Colony of South Australia* (Adelaide, W.C. Cox, 1862) pp. 98–99.
61. Robert Richard Torrens, *An Essay on the Transfer of Title by Registration* (London: Cassell, Petter, Galpin & Co: 1882) p. 54.
62. "Enhancing the Marketability of Land: The Suit to Quiet Title Source," *The Yale Law Journal*, Vol. 68, No. 6 (May, 1959), p. 1245.
63. South Australia Certificates of Title Registry, Book 1, folios 150 and 242; Book V, folio 20; Book VIII, folio 188; Book X, folio 20, Book XVI, folio 141.
64. Torrens, *Essay on the Transfer of Title*, p. 37.

References

Adelaide Times.

Book of Regulations for Disposing of Land in South Australia.

First Annual Report of the Colonization Commissioners for South Australia.

Fourth Annual Report of the Colonization Commission.

Historical Records of Australia. Series I, Governors' Despatches to and from England.

Outline of a Plan of a Proposed Colony to be Founded on the South Coast of Australia, with an Account of the Soil, Climate, Rivers, etc.

Registration of Deeds Act, 5 Vic. No. 8.

South Australia Act, 4 and 5 William IV, c. 95.

South Australia Gazette and Colonial Register.

South Australia Parliamentary Debates, 1857–1858.

South Australian Register.

Waste Lands Acts, 5&4 Victoria, Ch 36, sections VII, VIII, XI; 9&10 Victoria, Ch 104, sections I, IV; 18&19 Victoria ch 56, sections 2, 8, 9.

Enhancing the Marketability of Land: The Suit to Quiet Title Source. 1959. *The Yale Law Journal* 68 (6): 1245–1317.

Bennett, James. 1843. *Historical and Descriptive Account of South Australia*. London: Smith, Elder & Co.

Dutton, Francis. 1846. *South Australia and Its Mines, with an Historical Sketch of the Colony*. London: T. &W. Boone.

Evans, Matilda (Maud Jeanne Franc). 1911 [1867]. *Golden Gifts*. London: Sampson, Low, Marston & Co.

Foster, Robert, and Amanda Nettlebeck. 2018. *Out of the Silence: The History and Memory of South Australia's Frontier Wars*. Mile End: Wakefield Press.

Gouger, Robert. 1838. *South Australia in 1837 in a Series of Letters, with a Postscript from 1838*. London: Harvey and Darton.

Grey, George. 1841. *Journals of Two Expeditions of Discovery in North-West and Western Australia, During the Years 1837, 38 and 39*. London: T. & W, Boone.

Grguric, Nicolas K. 2007. *Fortified Homesteads: The Architecture of Fear in Frontier South Australia and the Northern Territory, ca 1847–1885*. PhD dissertation, Flinders University.

Harrison, Robert. 1862. *Colonial Sketches or Five Years in South Australia*. London: Hall, Virtue and Co.

Hodder, Edwin. 1891. *George Fife Angas, Father and Founder of South Australia*. London: Hodder and Stoughton.

Hubbe, Ulrich. 1857. *The Voice of Reason and History Brought to Bear Against the Present Absurd and Expensive Method of Transferring and Encumbering Immovable Property*. Adelaide, cited in Antonio Esposito. 2003. Ulrich Hubbe's Role in the Creation of the 'Torrens System' of Land Registration in South Australia. *Adelaide Law Review* 24: 284.

Hunter, James. "Ville de Bordeaux," SA History Hub, History Trust of South Australia. http://sahistoryhub.com.au/things/ville-de-bordeaux

Llewellyn-Smith, Michael. 2012. *Behind the Scenes: The Politics of Planning Adelaide*. Adelaide: University of Adelaide Press.

Phillips, Willard. 1828. *Manual of Political Economy*. Boston: Hilliard, Gray, Little & Wilkins.

Pike, Douglas. 1961. Introduction of the Real Property Act in South Australia. *Adelaide Law Review* 1 (2): 169–189.

Simmonds, P.L. 1875. The Ethnological Collection at the International Exhibition. *Journal of the Society for Arts* 22 (1134): 821.

Stephens, John. 1839. *The History of the Rise and Progress of the New British Province of South Australia*. 2nd ed. London: Smith, Elder & Co.

Torrens, Robert. 1838. *Plan of an Association in Aid of the Irish Poor Law*. London: Longman, Orme.

Torrens, Robert Richard. 1859. *The South Australian System of Conveyancing by Registration of Title*. Adelaide: Register and Observer Printing Offices.

———. 1882. *An Essay on the Transfer of Title by Registration*. London: Cassell, Petter, Galpin & Co.

Wakefield, Edward Gibbon. 1829. *A Letter from Sydney, the Principal Town of Australasia*. London: J. Cross.

———. 1833. *England and America, a Comparison of the Social and Political State of Both Nations*. London: Richard Bentley.

Whalan, Douglas J. Torrens, Sir Robert Richard 1814–1884. *Australian Dictionary of Biography*. National Centre of Biography, Australian National University. http://adb.anu.edu.au/biography/torrens-sir-robert-richard-4739/text7869

Woods, James Dominick. 1879. *The Native Tribes of South Australia*. Adelaide: E.S. Wigg & Co.

CHAPTER 5

Registration: Erasing Indigenous Land Rights

Abstract Land title registration on Torrens' model spread quickly, not only to other settler colonies in Australia, New Zealand, and western Canada, but also to colonies where indigenous peoples' land tenure ideas and practices did not accommodate plantation agriculture, commercial timber operations, or mining. Registration in the Philippines and Malaysia, both of which adopted Torrens' system, erased those traditional land rights concepts, while the system in Fiji (in addition to incompletely understanding traditional tenure approaches) became a way of isolated indigenous people from a plantation system. The African experience suggests registration became a tool used by an elite with access to the mechanisms of state power to maintain traditional control over rural populations.

Keywords Land title registration • Torrens system • Philippines • Malaysia • Fiji • Colonialism

As far back as anyone could remember, Mateo Carino, his father, and his father's father had controlled their clan's grassy fields at Kafagway, up in the pine forests of the mountain backbone of Luzon island in the Philippines. But the American officials and businessmen hastening to the islands after the Spanish American war were already eyeing the highlands—never completely subdued in three centuries of Spanish rule—as a

D. Ress, *Deeds, Titles, and Changing Concepts of Land Rights*,
https://doi.org/10.1007/978-3-030-64191-7_5

temperate haven from tropical heat. Kafagway was particularly intriguing because of the dribbling of gold from the Igorot peoples' panning and small open pit mines and the myths of still greater riches in the hills. The year after Carino held the region on behalf of the rebel leader Emilio Aguinaldo, he agreed to sell some 146 hectares of land at Kafagway to an American named Metcalf A. Clarke, for 6000 pesos. Carino's rights over that land, where 20 families built their homes and corrals for their cattle, derived from his leadership of a clan of the Ibaloi (usually translated as the people who live in houses). His ability to grant rights of access to the land was clear enough to him and, at least initially, to Clarke, as he busily amassed mineral claims in the region.

But the year after Carino and Clarke struck their deal, the new American colonial government created a land registration court, on the pattern of South Australia's land title office. The year after that, in 1903, the colonial government decreed that Kafagway and the lands around it would be a military reservation. To secure his rights, Clarke needed Carino's title to the land to be registered, so that Clarke's purchase could stand against any claim from the government. When Carino tried, the colonial government opposed his request, and later justified its stance by telling the colonial high court (and later the US Supreme Court) that Carino was a member of a savage tribe, that such tribes did not own land and that the land in question belonged to the state.[1] Clarke's efforts to register title to land would test a new imperial power's understanding of the place of individuals on land. The end result, thanks to framing of the question that Torrens title forced, would be a confirmation of fee simple ownership for a society that had found other ways of living on its land.

Torrens' land title system would spread rapidly from South Australia. Adopted within just a couple of years by the settlers of other Australian colonies, as well as in New Zealand and British Columbia, it also captured the attention of administrators of colonies where large indigenous populations with laws and customs about rights to land that did not easily accommodate would-be investors in plantation agriculture and mining. American officials in the Philippines imposed Torrens's title registration system in 1902. British officials adopted it for the Federated Malay States (Perak, Selangor, Negri Sembilan, and Pahang) in 1897 (initially for parcels of 100 acres or more). Colonial officials imposed the system in the state of Johor; Kedah, Kelantan, Perlis and Terengganu adopted it beginning in 1912.

What had started as a way to quickly declare title to land that in official eyes belonged to nobody because it belonged only to Australian Aborigines would shortly become a way to take land that belonged to colonized people—peoples who a Locke or Winthrop would say had property rights to land because they were cultivating it. On the other hand, one of the first colonial governments to adopt the system after its spread across Australia—Fiji—did so in a deliberate effort to preserve what officials perceived as customary land tenure. In a similar way, when the US Supreme Court overturned Philippines Supreme Court Justice Charles Willard's ruling and held that Carino did in fact have valid title to the land, it seemed to be creating space for traditional notions of land rights. Why neither the Fiji colonial officials' nor the American high court's supposed care for those traditional ideas about land would prove to be effective is the subject of this chapter. Title registration in Torrens's system, much like Massachusetts-style deed recordation tended to entrench fee simple ownership and nullify any other approach to rights to use land and the natural resources it contains.

The question is whether the failure of those officials or those Supreme Court justices to protect those unfamiliar rights to land was an effect of the process of registering title or whether something else (or additional) was at issue. Ahmad Ibrahim and Judith Sihombing note that in Torrens's system "equity had no place"—that is, the kind of legal proceeding that ends with a judicial order requiring a person or institution to do "that which ought to be done" (as legal commentators commonly put it.)[2] The idea of Torrens's system instead is that the most efficient resolution of disputes over rights to any piece of land was best accomplished through strict enforcement of an administrative process. A rules-based, relatively mechanical system to validate title to land is less open—in fact, not open at all—to any complex of parallel or overlapping rights to land. Western legal scholars make exactly this point when they cite the way the rules of Torrens's title registration bar consideration of constructive notice doctrine. That doctrine includes the "should have known" or "could not have known" notions that can upset land deals if, say, it is a group of heirs rather than a single one who own land, or if the second purchaser of land, unaware it had already been sold, wins the race to the courthouse to record ownership.[3] Constructive notice could, perhaps, be an issue in validating title to land where, say, a community had for many generations recognized use rights to hunt in the forests around a Malaysian village or to pan for gold in a Philippine stream.

The essentially automatic functioning of the Torrens system was therefore particularly attractive to officials in colonies with large indigenous populations holding differing views on land tenure. It could also be particularly disquieting in communities where there was a consensus that land tenure ought naturally to be in the nature of ownership—Blackstone's "sole and despotic dominion which one man claims and exercises over the external things of the world, in total exclusion of the right of any other individual in the universe." In most American states and in Britain itself there remained a strong sense that when claims to land conflict, resolving them ought to be at least as much a matter of equity as of documentation. [4] "To determine the adverse claims of parties touching their right in things, judicial process is indispensable," Ohio Supreme Court Justice John Allen Shauck wrote, overturning the state's 1896 law establishing a Torrens system.[5] Other challenges to Torrens registration laws came in Illinois, Minnesota, and Massachusetts, each arguing that the system deprived individuals of their property without due process (by giving land title registrars judicial powers reserved by state and federal constitutions to the courts). The high courts in those states, however, did not follow Justice Shauck's lead.[6] Those states, taking a lesson from Ohio, had enacted laws that did not make registration mandatory and provided for appeal to state appellate courts, which was intended to moot the constitutional argument. Ultimately, the US Supreme Court upheld the Massachusetts law, essentially settling the matter. It did so, however, on procedural grounds with a narrow 5-4 decision—not ruling on whether state officials had improperly denied property owners due process, but simply saying that in the dispute that question could have been resolved by an appeal to the local circuit court. (The issue was whether the registration of a lot purchased by a Chelsea, Massachusetts, lawyer, and his store-owner business partner properly recorded the boundary line with one neighbor.)[7]

Justice Shauck's legal practice had focused on the complexities of settling large estates and handling testamentary trusts and fiduciary affairs, the area of property law perhaps most affected by Torrens's system. His concern was the way that Torrens system registration focused simply on land, rather than on the relationship of individuals to land. "The substantial thing determined by registration is that the person who makes the application has a right of property in the land to the exclusion of all other persons," he wrote. The issue of rights to land was an attribute of a person, not of a thing, for "The land is not a thing of shifting situs like a ship, against which obligations may accrue today in one jurisdiction and tomorrow in another," Shauck noted.[8] This distinction between the locus of a claim—thing or person—was, Shauck continued, how the US Supreme Court sorted out disputed titles to land in the Iowa Half Breed Tract, when it held that the recorded deeds in the Lee County court house validated land rights (and at the same time declined to restore the rights to occupy and use the land as a commons, as the 1824 treaty creating the Tract had directed).[9]

Nor would Mateo Carino and his clan continue to share the land at Kafagway after his posthumous Supreme Court victory. That decision simply cleared the way for him to sell the 146 hectares. To be sure, that was the idea from the start, when the buyer, Metcalf Clarke, asked the Philippines Court of Land Registration to inscribe Carino as owner of the land. Clarke worried that his two-year-old agreement for the land might come to nothing because Governor General William Taft was already thinking of the mountain hamlet, with its "air as bracing as the Adirondacks" as a possible summer capital for the tropical colony.[10] The land registration court issued a formal title to the land when Clarke, supposedly acting on Carino's behalf, declared that Carino had been in possession of the land when the two men struck their deal. When the colonial government challenged this grant in the Court of First Instance for Benguet Province, that court voided the registration.[11] Carino, through Clarke, then appealed, arguing that the former Spanish colonial government had, in effect, granted his rights to the land from "immemorial use and occupation."[12] This mattered, because the United States had promised to recognize Spanish colonial land grants, while also insisting that ungranted land was deemed to be in the public domain, to be disposed of as the new colonial government felt appropriate. But to presume a Spanish grant by virtue of continued use and occupation was wrong, Philippines Supreme Court Justice Charles Willard ruled, writing that:

> Here the surrounding circumstances are incompatible with the existence of a grant, It is known that for nearly three hundred years all attempts to convert the Igorots of the Province of Benguet to the Christian religion completely failed, and that during that time they remained practically in the same condition as they were when the Islands were first occupied by the Spaniards.[13]

Carino and his people, therefore, were not protected by any Spanish laws relating to the granting or sale or use of public land, since all land not granted by the Spanish colonial government was public land, with only the government empowered to hold or sell it. While the United States had agreed to recognize earlier grants, it also assumed the Spanish crown's rights to the rest of the islands' lands.[14] Moreover, looking at Carino's land soon after the war with Spain and the Philippine insurgency had ended (and before many of the Igorot had felt able to safely return) it was clear that "No one has lived upon it for many years. It was never used for anything but pasturage of animals," Willard wrote, adding "it has apparently not been used by the petitioner for any purpose."[15]

Cultivation—John Locke's infusion of labor that created a right of property in land—was still enough of theoretical basis for a claim to rights to land that Willard felt it important to scotch that argument. Similarly, the fact that Carino, by then spending much of his time in Manila as a representative of the highlands region in the governor's office (and a regular irritant to American officials), was not using the land at the time did not assure him of any squatter's right or adverse possession claim. Willard made a nod to Blackstone's definition of customary law and the space that common law reserved for custom dating from time immemorial. But he went on to suggest that Carino had undermined that kind of claim because he had sought to obtain title from the Spanish colonial government in 1894. The judge did not think it mattered that Carino had acted in response to a decree that all agricultural land on which a customary right or right derived from longstanding possession had not been officially acknowledged would revert to the crown. (Carino also tried in 1896, although Willard seems to have been unaware of this; nothing came of it, apparently because the Spanish authorities were eyeing the land as a site for a sanatorium).[16] To close off any other path to a claim of title, Willard also carefully noted that forest lands, like those where the Igorot planted their swidden fields or dug for gold had always been crown lands under the Spanish.[17]

But the idea that the state's sovereignty might override private possession of land bothered US Supreme Court Justice Oliver Wendall Holmes. He began his opinion overturning Willard's ruling with the sharply worded comment that "The acquisition of the Philippines was not for the purpose of acquiring the lands occupied by the inhabitants." The property rights of "one who actually owned land for many years cannot be deprived of it for failure to comply with certain ceremonies prescribed either by the acts of the Philippine Commission or by Spanish law," Holmes continued.[18] The justice, after reviewing the record, wrote that Carino and his ancestors had "held the land as owners" for more than 50 years before the cessions of the Philippines to the United States by the Treaty of Paris, for

> His grandfather had lived upon it, and had maintained fences sufficient for the holding of cattle, according to the custom of the country, some of the fences, it seems, having been of much earlier date. His father had cultivated parts and had used parts for pasturing cattle, and he had used it for pasture in his turn. They all had been recognized as owners by the Igorots, and he had inherited or received the land from his father in accordance with Igorot custom.[19]

Here, Holmes transformed the rights of occupation, use, and management of clan land that Carino, like his father and grandfather, had exercised as clan leader into rights of ownership. Ownership was the connection of people to place that Holmes understood best and that had come to seem the most normal state to many Americans. When he ruled that the US assumption of sovereignty over the Philippines was not about removing people from land they occupied, he automatically framed indigenous individuals' tenure as ownership in severalty; that is, an exclusive right to occupy, use, and control access by others. American power was (thanks to Holmes' subtle, perhaps unconscious eliding of the difference between living on land and owning it) focused on protecting the Filipino people by protecting their rights of property, however incompletely understood.

That protection included recognizing an individual's holding of land "as far back as testimony or memory goes," as Holmes wrote in his own echoing of Blackstone's definition of customary law. He flipped on its head the colonial government's argument that Carino's people, "as a savage tribe" never brought under Spanish colonial rule could have any title to land since "The argument to that effect seems to amount to a denial of native titles … for the want of ceremonies which the Spaniards would not have permitted and had not the power to enforce."[20] Unlike Mr. Rowle's recorded deeds, Torrens system registration could protect indigenous land rights, or so Holmes suggested here. "Whatever consideration may have been shown to the North American Indians, the dominant purpose of the whites in America was to occupy the land," Holmes wrote. "No one, we suppose, would deny that … our first object in the internal administration of the islands is to do justice to the natives, not to exploit their country for private gain."[21]

Despite Holmes' sentiment about protecting the rights of the people of the Philippines, the decision did, in fact, clear the way for removing Carino's people from the land, a not-unexpected consequence of not really seeing the nature of customary rights. Carino died the year before Holmes' ruling, and his own family did not regain their rights on clan land. Nor did the clan itself. A century later, the Philippines National Commission on Indigenous Peoples rejected claims of Carino's great-grandchildren to about half the land on which Carino wanted to register a title of ownership. It did, however, award a certificate of ancestral land title to a family claiming a right to land derived from Carino's wife. (The Igorot recognized both patrilineal and matrilineal rights of inheritance of use and management rights to land.)[22] The land, in any event, remains as of this writing in the control of the Philippines government, although squatters have occupied portions.[23] Clarke, whose Benguet Consolidated Mining Co. started operating an ore-processing mill while continuing the court battle over title registration, lost control of the enterprise as well as his fortune when a storm in 1911 destroyed that plant and flooded the company's mine. (The mine was actually located on land to the east of Carino's on which Clarke also had obtained mineral rights.) Clarke died in poverty, but the new investors ended up with what would become one of the largest gold mines of the interwar years, and one that in the quarter century after Holmes' ruling would pay dividends totaling 30.5 million pesos—roughly 15,000 times what Clarke had paid for Carino's land.[24]

When Holmes affirmed an American interest in protecting native peoples—at least those who, unlike Native Americans, weren't in the way of his nation's dominant purpose—American interest in the Pacific had been growing for some time: sandalwood and *beche-de-mer* for the Chinese market had attracted traders to South Pacific islands from early nineteenth century. Land and indigenous peoples' land rights would become an issue here, however. An urgent search for cheap land for plantation-style production of tropical or subtropical crops brought adventurers from both the United States and Australia to the Fiji islands when the American Civil War cut global supply of cotton. Land, it seemed, could be had in exchange for some liquor or firearms on islands with no recognizable state authority or court to say no. A quick crop with minimal investment in order to feed a market where prices were soaring seemed too good an opportunity to resist. But as settlers pushed farther into the interior of the island of Viti Levu, the Kai Colo clans fought back and were only subdued with the arrival of British troops. Britain annexed the islands in 1874 and moved quickly to bring order to the question of land and labor with two key steps. The first was to protect Fijians from further encroachment. The second: to make legitimate the landholdings of European settlers. This latter was most easily done through Torrens' land title registration.[25]

The new government aimed to calm conflict by forbidding further sales of land by Fijians and by promising to look at whether European settlers had in fact a legitimate right to land they claimed they bought. But before the colonial government could, under Torrens' system, certify the validity of a purchase of land, it had to be certain of the seller's title. In South Australia, this ultimately went back to the crown. There, the Colonization Commission acted, in effect, as agent, responsible both for arranging sales to settlers and, supposedly, protecting Aboriginal land rights—rights which, however, were not seen as including an owner's right to forbid access. Fijian rights seemed much less clear. Supposed experts were little help. William Pritchard, the first British Consul in Fiji, said all land on the island was owned by families. But the tribe retained an interest, with its collective rights to the land appertaining to the chief. The sale of any parcel of land was only possible after a collective decision by the tribe, through the chief and heads of families. However, as the new Land Claims Commission would soon learn, in the southern part of Viti Levu, where the leading chief, Ratu Kini Nanova, had handled all sales whites in this thickly settled region, his "position and right to sell lands on this part of the coast is unquestioned." On Vanau Levu island, meanwhile, the ruling chief, Tui Cakau, "never consulted the *taukeis* (holders of land) before selling," leading the commission to wonder whether those sales were legitimate.[26] The Australian missionary Lorimer Fison said individuals held land but that they could not sell it or be dispossessed. "In fact they consider their title to be inextinguishable as long as they themselves are not extinguished. It may be held in abeyance, but it cannot be destroyed, he wrote."[27]

Arthur Gordon, appointed Fiji's second governor the year after annexation, convened a council of chiefs to discuss the land question in 1876. At that council, Tui Bua said his people were not planting coconuts because of their confusion over land rights. Gordon suggested allocating land to individuals, but after much discussion the chiefs eventually proposed a division among occupying families with the families then having the option to allot parcels to individual or to hold the land in as a single family tract, or to align with others to create a tribal holding.[28] When they gathered again the next year, the chiefs were unable to ratify even this apparently fairly flexible model. There was, it turned out, no single archipelago-wide tradition to adopt. At the 1878 council, again considering land tenure tradition the chief Roko Tui Ba proposed apportioning land to *tokatoka* family units. Roko Tui Bua replied "We have no divisions amongst us called Tokatoka." Tui Ba then suggested division among the *mataqali* (the clan), adding that it "is firm, and ancient, and understood by everyone," while Ratu Marika interjected if land were registered to clans "there will always be trouble and disputes."[29] Nevertheless, that was the approach the colonial government adopted, despite indications that some Fijian communities allotted land to individuals or families and some simply to chiefs with authority over several clans.

The Land Claims Commission eventually validated less than half the settlers' claims. On the standard theory of the day that there was no individual landholding in chiefdoms, the commission held that even those Europeans who had paid Fijian chiefs for land had not necessarily acquired title to land. (Title was even more dubious for those settlers who had simply swapped guns or liquor or other goods with whomever they found on the land that they wanted, in the commission's view.) A critical question was whether a settler had paid the chief as if he himself had an individual right of ownership or as agent for a group of individuals holding rights to communal land.[30] Here, the commission seemed ready to act almost like court of equity (as opposed to merely administrative application of a rule). It held hearings to investigate the nature of various communities' chiefly authority, any claims to that authority as well as what rights to what lands were held by whom.

If the commission found that a chief had authority to determine rights to community land and had not exceeded that authority in selling land it then ruled on whether the buyer had paid a fair price. This would be the basis for overturning many transactions, denying settlers and plantation operators title to land. The commission also required that the buyer either lives on the land or has established a plantation on it.[31] With that, the commission shrugged off the usual concern of a proceeding in equity: finding a just solution to a conflict of claims when the formalities of statute, administrative regulation, or court precedent did not provide clarity or expedient resolution. Instead of looking to restore the status of land before an unfair or misunderstood or fraudulent transaction, the commission here focused on what was equitable after a questionable deal gave a settler or plantation owner possession.[32]

The end result was a division of the colony's territory into two types of land. One was "freehold" land, registered with the commission, owned, occupied, and exploited by white settlers and investors, which could be freely bought and sold. The other was, "native land," owned by a *mataqali*, which could not sell its land. "By Fijian custom, that is by Fijian law, the absolute alienation of land as understood by us was unknown, and, therefore, strictly speaking, illegal," the commission concluded.[33] The colonial government's land policy was one of "complete laissez-faire to land in freehold ownership and a policy of rigid protectionism towards land in the ownership and occupation of the native Fijians," as a later director of lands put it.[34] It would become the foundation of a racial and social policy.

Unlike Justice Holmes, with his certainty that individual ownership was normative, Gordon saw a linkage between customary land tenure—which he concluded was communal—and political control on islands with a history of violent resistance to European settlers and government. The connection was through the chiefs' power to who could use and live on communal land. Gordon also linked individuals' economic and political roles with their ethnicity, while at the same time seeking to end the forced employment of Fijians on European plantations.[35] This role, instead, was to be performed by Indian immigrants, who were to be landless. Plantation land and the capital required for large-scale sugar production (the staple plantation owners moved to after the collapse of cotton prices) were to be owned by Europeans, with their landholding secured by the Torrens title registration system. Indian indentured workers provided the labor. Fijians were to live on and use their land in traditional ways, outside the colony's economic connection to the rest of the world. Economic reality required plantations; a self-congratulatory assumption of an obligation to a supposedly more primitive people was the reason for limiting individual rights on native lands.

Still farther outside both the land system and political system were children of European traders or settlers and Fijian women. Their demand for a place on the land and, therefore, in colonial society was one final pressure point constraining a desired expansion of plantation agriculture, particularly in the area around the colonial capital of Suva and the province of Rewa. So Jimmy Dyer, the "half-caste, son of James S. Dyer," a whaler who left his ship to settle in Rewa, argued to the commission that he had inherited a right to native land because his father had been given land and chiefly status, marked by gifts of yams. Commissioner Walter Carew, impatient with a continued resistance to European land acquisition that took the form of destroying property boundary markers, declared flatly that it was "beyond belief, and impossible" that Dyer senior could have received such chiefly tribute. His son's claim was disallowed.[36]

A Creole man with a reputation as a brutal overseer also failed in his bid to hold land he had registered. He had claimed ownership through a sugar cane sale agreement, registered as a land title because it provided for a grant of a right of way if the full value of the sugar was not paid. The Supreme Court of Fiji rejected this argument, holding that although the Registrar had recorded the agreement as a lien on a title, it was in fact not a document memorializing a transfer of land. Since the overseer was attempting to secure title to land owned by the Colonial Sugar Refining Co. but that was apparently a hamlet for people, like him, who were of neither Fijian nor fully European, he seems to have little chance of luck.[37] In a 1908 decision, the high court ruled that even if title were issued in error, it could not overturn it. The Fijian ordinance was clear. It declared that the "certificate of title issued by the Registrar" was "conclusive evidence that the person named therein as proprietor of the land is the absolute and indefeasible owner thereof."[38]

In the United States, the similarly marginal political position of the children and grandchildren of Native American women and white traders and trappers, as well as the ambivalent nature of "Indian title" treaty rights they were granted to the Half Breed Tracts of Minnesota and Nebraska, seemed impossible to resolve by recordation, after the controversies and corruption of the dissolution of the Iowa Half Breed Tract discussed in Chap. 3. Here, the resolution was to adopt variations on the warrants granting contingent rights to land that Virginia had used as a war financing technique and that the United States adopted as an inexpensive way of rewarding ex-soldiers. The scrip and allotment certificates granted to treaty rights holders allowed for the transformation of a still never-defined right to a specific piece of land into cash or a fee simple title. Almost all were cashed in. This was also the case with scrip issued to resolve land claims of Lake Superior Chippewa bands, the Choctaw of Mississippi and children of Ponca and Pawnee women and white fathers.[39]

Torrens' registration system also seemed to provide a way to overturn indigenous land rights as British investors eyed the resources of the Malay peninsula. There, as colonial official William Maxwell would write, "Land is abundant, but … there is no restriction upon the selection and appropriation of forest land." Even when forest land was not occupied, it might still be subject to an absolute proprietary claim if fruit trees remained on it, a headache for logging and would be plantation firms. In response, the colonial government moved in 1880 to try to bring a new order to the tangle of land rights claims.[40] Sent to South Australia to study Torrens's system, Maxwell came back with the notion that any country's land ultimately belonged to its sovereign and that the sovereign—whether that was the Crown in South Australia or the Sultan of Selangor, for who Maxwell would write a Torrens style land title law. That meant the sovereign was properly the one to validate rights to land, which clearly helped win over the Sultan, as well as those colonial officials looking to grant and tax timber, mining, and plantation concessions.[41] Torrens style land registration systems were eventually adopted in the rest of the Federated Malay States, but the option of registering small holdings was rarely taken up. A standard certificate of title could not easily be adopted to reflect the kind of land rights secured by a couple of fruit trees planted deep in a forest. The relatively high fees for registering and surveying smaller parcels meant few transfers of less than 100 acres were registered. Few communities actively exercising traditional rights to land, when that land was not eyed by a would-be plantation owner or mining firm, ever thought to register it.[42]

Torrens, after all, had used the model of the shipping registry, designed to disclose who was ultimately responsible for the financial obligations a vessel and crew incurred to something—land—that that he saw as essentially another form of capital. The aim was to avoid or expedite legal disputes over ownership of land as well as to secure the interests of creditors who had lent money secured by land. It was not until 1996, when the Johor state government moved to evict indigenous Jakun families from the proposed site of a dam and reservoir, that Malaysian courts confirmed customary rights to land—in this case, traditional rights to forage on some 22,000 hectares in the Sungai Linggiu valley. Justice Moktar Sidin concluded that evicted families had relied on their ability to forage on the land, as their ancestors had, and did so following traditional practices. Common law, he wrote "recognizes native land rights, even in countries practicing the Torrens land system" including " the right to live on their land as their forefathers had lived … even the future generations of the aboriginal people would be entitled to this right of their forefathers."[43]

Justice Moktar pushed aside the curtain that the title registrar closes—the principle that state certification of ownership rights to land fixes the moment at which those rights begin.[44] It is, on the face of things, unlike the Massachusetts-style recordation system which emphasizes the history of the chain of ownership. With recordation, it is the ability to trace each link in a public record, and if necessary to test it in court, that confirms ownership rights.[45] In much of the United States, which has shunned the Torrens system in favor of recordation, the issue is somewhat mooted, since this history starts with a grant of a portion of the public domain through a patent issued by the General Land Office. The theory here is the same that underlies Torrens' (and Maxwell's in Selangor): namely that the land was the State's to grant. In both instances, whether in South Australia or South Dakota, the Crown or the General Land Office intervened between the native people on the land and the individuals seeking ownership rights—the rights, that is, not only to use and occupy but most importantly to exclude others from land and to be able to sell it.

In one corner of Colorado (one of the few states to briefly adopt the Torrens system), however, a conflict of rights was resolved—with the use rights of older residents dismissed—through the mechanics of Torrens title registration. The issue arose in the high, lean country of the Rio Grande headwaters, the San Luis valley of Costilla County. There, generations of Spanish-speaking settlers had held a variety of rights, from exclusive use of plots of the valley's more fertile land to shared use rights to pasture in *dehesa* (grassland with isolated trees) and access to the commons of the *monte* (mountains) for timber and fuel. They had first come to this land thanks to an enormous, one-million-plus acre *empresario* grant to an American resident of the then-Mexican town of Taos, Stephen Lee, and the 13-year-old son of his French-Canadian brother-in-law. Lee had promised to settle Mexican peasants on the grant. The idea was that such settlement would discourage American immigrants from seizing control of what was at the time Mexican territory occupied only by the wandering Kapota band of the Ute nation.[46] After the 13-year-old's death during an uprising by American adventurers in Taos, his father bought out Lee, won a confirmation of the grant of some 900,000 acres of the valley from Congress.

At the same time, the grantee transferred some of the commons, as commons, to the towns that the Mexican settlers had established in the valley. After his death, his heirs sold the land that remained to the territorial governor of Colorado, William Gilpin, who confirmed the settlers' various use rights.[47] Gilpin and his successors began selling off portions of the grant, through conveyances carefully documenting the use rights of the settlers and eventually their descendants, noting the sales were "subject to claims of the local people by prescription or otherwise to right to pasture, wood, and lumber and so-called settlements right in, to and upon said land."[48] But after buying some 77,000 acres of the grant in 1960, North Carolina lumber company owner Jack Taylor filed suit in federal court for permission to extinguish those claims by registering the land under Colorado's Torrens act. Taylor also fenced off the land and set up locked gates on the paths to pasture commons.[49]

A federal appeals court confirmed Taylor's title, but also held the settlers' descendants retained rights to go onto the commons and let their animals graze there because they'd done so for so long without challenge.[50] Two decades after Taylor's purchase, the conflict resumed with a state court action in which the settlers' descendants sought a formal title to the commons, arguing that Taylor's Torrens title was invalid because of inadequate notice to rights holders. Taylor argued that his Torrens title cleared the slate of anyone else's claim to any rights to his land. The Costilla County District Court judge agreed.[51] On appeal, the Colorado Supreme Court upheld Taylor's argument that under the state Torrens Act once a title certificate is issued, individuals "may ascertain all matters related to the validity of the title from the certificate alone." While this seemed to shoot down the settler descendants' case, the high court also found that Taylor had not followed the act's notice requirements.[52] It would take another two decades of legal skirmishing, however, before the Colorado Supreme Court confirmed the use rights of some of the settler descendants.[53] More than four decades after Taylor set in motion the mechanics of title registration to erase the settler descendants' rights to use the land, a court finally ordered open the gates he had installed to block access to his mountain meadows and woods.

In this drama—a classic cowboy story melodrama of the rich outsider closing off the land on which hard-working families depend—it is striking how compelling the urge to rely on an administrative process, summarized in a standardized document of state, had been. In the face of more than a century-old pattern of land use and rights, elaborated in a way that recognized the different qualities and potentialities of particular portions of the valley, simple declaration in Taylor's certificate of title matched the simpler view of a wider society, unconcerned with the valley itself, of the nature of land.

What, really, can we read from a piece of paper, a certificate of title issued by the state or an instrument (revealing word, that) held by a Recorder of Deeds or entered into a courthouse deed book? Both registration and recordation brought the public at large into what in England at the time of their introduction was still a matter of private investigation: the question of who had what kind of property in land. In England, in fact, Torrens' South Australia innovation had, with much debate, inspired the Land Transfer Act of 1875. It sought to establish a national registry of land titles in England, but because registration was voluntary and because the registrar had broad discretion to validate or decline to recognize title, the system had little impact.[54] As Ohio Supreme Court Justice Shauck wrote, there was something unsettling about leaving such a fundamental question—the place of a person on the land—to an administrative process.

It was only when state laws provided for appeal of a registrar's issue of a title certificate and said landholders were not required to incur the relatively high fee for an initial Torrens title certificate that a handful of American states accepted a parallel Torrens system for recording title. Colorado was one of the fourteen states that had retained a Torrens system by 1960, when Taylor obtained his certificate, but it was not one of the three where the system was used by a more than insignificant number of purchasers in a handful of large cities.[55] "By a simple change in land transfer, land is to become liquid and credits established … what else can be meant by those who urge that land should be as easily transferable as a ship or a share of stock or an automobile?" wrote Iowa law professor Percy Bordwell, arguing against a renewal of interest in Torrens title in the wake of the failure of four New York title insurance companies during the 1930s. "Land is not as liquid as a share of stock and never will be. It is essentially a local commodity," Bordwell added. He noted that even in Chicago, where Torrens registration had been an option since 1897, the supposed enhanced security and value a Torrens title was supposed to provide had not led to a single parcel in the Loop, the city's skyscraper-studded financial and commercial center being registered.[56]

American indifference toward Torrens registration came despite the impassioned arguments of advocates, focused in part on the paperwork burden of, for example, the 24,000 deeds recorded in Boston in 1890 that prompted attorney John T. Hassam to argue that "the present system, cumbersome and unwieldy at best, is fairly breaking down of its own weight." To validate title to land, Hassam continued "necessitates long and exhaustive searches of a mass of records which are continually becoming more and more enormous, the tedious preparation of abstracts, disputes over titles, difficulties, delays, expense, examinations and re-examinations without end."[57] (Hassam did not complain about the wordiness and redundancies of language in those deeds, however.) That long process "is often fatal to an otherwise ready sale," complained

Chicago real estate broker M.M. Yeakle. "Delay suggests doubt of indefeasibility of title to a would-be purchaser ... As the law now stands—speaking generally—no man can be sure that he is the owner of land, unless he can show that he has paid for it, and has it in possession under a deed of record; but also, that his deed is the last link in an unbroken chain of properly drawn, executed and recorded conveyances ... if a single link is defective or missing, the title will fail of completeness—as far as the records are concerned."[58] The quirks of land law, particularly the notion that neglecting or delaying to record a deed might put a buyer at risk of losing land, created "the barbarous principle of caveat emptor," as Myres S. McDougal and John W. Brabner-Smith put it. "Darling of the courts on most occasions, he who here gets the judicial axe is the bona fide purchaser for value," the two lawyers contended.[59]

Recordation, however, would come to seem less burdensome largely thanks to improvements in indexing records as well as the role abstracters and insurers assumed in validating title and facilitating sales. The high cost of an initial registration discouraged American land buyers from opting for a Torrens title, in part because it involved exactly the same kind of research already performed in a title abstract and by conveyancing lawyer and in part because "the average land-owner does not desire to invite a lawsuit by seeking to register a title which he considers good, and that substantial lawsuits may arise from the attempt under a Torrens proceeding to fix definite boundary lines," Philadelphia lawyer Edward H. Cushman noted. "A title considered marketable might be found to be unmarketable if disturbed, whereas if permitted to remain dormant, the defect might be cured through lapse of time," Cushman wrote, adding: "Furthermore, the proceeding under the Torrens act merely registers good titles and does not cure defective ones."[60] Torrens certificates, moreover, not only erased histories of land rights—as alleged in Carino's and Dyers's cases as well as those of the Fijian Creole settlement and the San Luis Valley—but also risked nullifying the interests of future or potential rights-claimants, since certificates, once issued, were indefeasible title, which could be challenged in court only on the grounds of fraud or procedural error by the Registrar, critics like Bordwell and Richard R. Powell argued. "The important thing to bear in mind is that the logic of registration of title is a revolution in our land law. More is involved than mere changes in methods of transfer" since "only a 'good holding title' and not a 'marketable title' is necessary for registration as an 'absolute title,'" Bordwell wrote.[61]

For at least some jurists and colonial officials, the essential effect of Torrens title was a "transference of primary attention from the mobile, mortal, mistakable persons temporarily possessing or claiming rights over patches of the earth's surface, to the immovable, durable, precisely definable units of land affected and the adoption of these as the basis of record instead,"[62] the British colonial officials Ernest Dowson and V.L.O. Sheppard wrote. In a sense, proclaiming title to land makes land legible in ways it had not been before, as Hall, Hirsch, and Li argue, while the state's authority to certify title means property rights to natural resources are "intimately bound up with the exercise of power and authority" as Sikor and Lund point out.[63] "Land, in fact, becomes as to its title entirely like stock in a corporation: it is transferable only on the official books … the land always goes with the certificate," Harvard Law School professor Joseph H. Beale argued, taking a view about the real nature of land, as essentially an investment asset, that had become an economists' convention.[64] Or, as the Vanuatu Supreme Court put it: "The essential feature of any Torrens System is the indefeasibility of the title of the registered proprietor … the register is everything."[65]

Nevertheless, in practice in the United States, land also went (as Beale might say) with the recorded deed. Both Torrens' system and American deed recordation marked a significant change from the English system, under which investigation of title to land was a private matter, because there was no centralized record of land ownership. While the American records did not in and of themselves prove title beyond challenge, as a Torrens title certificate did, the two systems made clear the state had an interest in quiet title.[66] For the American record is a notice to the world "and all persons attempting to deal with the land are bound with notice," the prominent nineteenth century Chicago attorney and Illinois Republican stalwart James P. Root would write. Even a deed that had not been recorded "is binding on all parties dealing with the land if the grantee is in possession of the land; in fact, everybody is bound by whatever title a person has in actual possession, whether he discloses his title or not," Root continued.[67] That unrecorded deed might lead individuals disputing rights to a particular piece of land into court to become the kind of complication that American advocates of Torrens' system argued hung like a dark cloud over real estate dealings. But that really was not much of a cloud to Root. The unvoiced point underpinning Root's discussion of deed recordation and title abstracting is that the state had inserted itself into property dealings through deed recordation, even if less assertively than through a

Torrens title certification. Root would be more explicit when elaborating on one particular issue in title abstracting when discussing land once held by Native Americans, where "it may be said the government has always recognised some claim in the Indian, but it was a visionary claim, founded upon no solid basis." White settlers and speculators, he noted "have ever been ready to take the land without compensation." The rights that Native American of the time were asserting to the Black Hills country of South Dakota

> must be respected until such time as the government shall acquire the right to put the land in the market, which may be done by buying out the Indian title or driving them out, which the government is able to do as soon as the lamb shall roil the waters, and thus be in a position to put the land in market, and thereby acquire a title as good as any title in this country.[68]

Arguing futilely against a proposal to adopt Torrens' system in Virginia (the state only eliminated the barely used option for land dealing in 2019), Big Stone Gap, Va., attorney J.F. Bullitt said it would interfere with an effective practice of using recorded instruments to resolve land disputes in court in ways, Torrens title could frustrate fair settlement, in his view. But for conflicts over land rights in the Philippines or the Territory of Hawaii, which had also adopted Torrens' system after annexation by the United States, he continued,

> it would make no difference, for the whole question with reference to these latest additions to our country is that they shall be pacified, and it is immaterial how this is done, whether justly, whether by fraud or force or murder. The Torrens System may, therefore, be a beautiful scheme for these benighted islands. But Virginians cannot be pacified except with justice.[69]

To invoke the authority of the state, as Mr. Rowle understood when he would record—and, finally failed to record—his rights to his land meant more than simply allying yourself to power: it had come to mean assuming power: the power to exclude, the power to exploit and the power to realize a profit when you chose.

Notes

1. Mateo Cariño v. Insular Government of the Philippine Islands, 7 Phil 132, (Philippines Supreme Court, 1906) and on appeal at 212 U.S. 449 (US Supreme Court, 1909); Olivia M. Habana, "Gold Mining in Benguet to 1898," *Philippine Studies* Vol. 48, no. 4 (2000) pp. 455–487; "The Benguet Consolidated Mining Co." in *Port of Manila and other Phillippine Ports Year Book* (Manila: Manila Harbor Board, 1936) p. 23.
2. Tan Sri Datuk Professor Ahmad Ibrahim and Judith Sihombing, *The Centenary of the Torrens System in Malaysia* (Singapore and Kuala Lumpur: Malayan Law Journal, 1989) p. 96.
3. This point is stressed in Eustace J. Harvey, *Land Law and Registration of Title, A Comparison of the Old and New Ways of Transferring Land* (London: Longmans Green, 1910) pp. 194, 196–197; James Edward Hogg, *Registration of Title to Land throughout the Empire: A Treatise on the Law Relating to Warranty of Title to Land by Registration and Transactions with Registered Land in Australia, New Zealand, Canada, England, Ireland, West Indies, Malaya, etc.* (Toronto: Carswell, 1920); John L. McCormack, "Torrens and Recording: Land Title Assurance in the Computer Age," *William Mitchell Law Review*, Vol. 18, No. 1 (1992) pp. 61–129; Carol Rose, *Property and Persuasion: Essays on the History, Theory, and Rhetoric of Ownership* (Boulder: Westview Press, 1994), p. 208.
4. William Blackstone, *Commentaries on the Laws of England* (Chicago: University of Chicago, 1979 [1765]) Vol. II, p. 2.
5. State ex rel. Attorney Gen. v. Guilbert, 56 Ohio St. 575 (Ohio Supreme Court, 1897) at 610.
6. People v. Simon, 176 Ill. 165 (Illinois Supreme Court, 1898); State v. Westfall, 85 Minn. 437 (Minnesota Supreme Court, 1902) Tyler v Judges of the Court of Registration 151 Mass. 71 (Supreme Judicial Court of Massachusetts, 1900).
7. Tyler v Judges of the Court of Registration, 179 U.S. 405 (US Supreme Court, 1900) at 410.
8. State ex rel v Guilbert at 624.
9. Webster v Reid 52 U.S. 437 (US Supreme Court, 1850).
10. S.E. Kane, *Life and Death in Luzon or Thirty Years with the Philippine Head-Hunters* (New York: Grosset & Dunlap, 1933) p. 319.
11. Mateo Cariño v. Insular Government of the Philippine Islands, 7 Phil 132, at 133.
12. *Ibid.*
13. *Ibid.*, at 134.
14. *Ibid.*
15. *Ibid.*, at 135.

16. *Ibid.*, at 136.
17. *Ibid.*, at 137.
18. Carino v. Insular Government 212 US 449, at 450.
19. *Ibid.*, at 456.
20. *Ibid.*, at 458.
21. *Ibid.*, at 459.
22. "Ibaloi Chieftan Descendents Assail NCIP," *The Philippines Star* February 12 2010; "Ibaloi Family Cries Foul over Land Claim Mess," *Philippines Daily Inquirer*, February 13, 2010.
23. "Milking What's Left of the Baguio Dairy Farm," *Philippines Daily Inquirer*, August 17 2016.
24. "The Benguet Consolidated Mining Co.," p. 23.
25. Gerald R. Ward, "Land Use and Land Alienation in Fiji to 1885," *Journal of Pacific History*, Vol. 4 (1969), pp. 3–25; Bruce Knapman, *Fiji's Economic History, 1874–1939: Studies of Capitalist Colonial Development* (Canberra: National Centre for Development Studies, Research School of Pacific Studies, Australian National University, 1987).
26. W.T. Pritchard, *Polynesian Reminiscences; or, Life in the South Pacific Islands* (London: Chapman, & Hall, 1866) p. 243: Lands Claims Commission Report 107a; Report 862 cited in Annelise Riles, "The Empty Place: Legal Formalities and the Cultural State" in The Place of Law (editors): Austin Sarat, Lawrence Douglas, Martha Merrill Umphrey (Ann Arbor: University of Michigan Press, 2003) pp. 48, 54.
27. Lorimer Fison, *Land Tenure in Fiji*. (London: Harrison, 1881) p. 12.
28. *Notes of the Proceedings of a Native Council* 1876, p. 22.
29. *Notes of the Proceedings of a Native Council* 1878, p. 53.
30. Peter France, *Charter of the Land: Custom and Colonisation In Fiji* (Oxford: Oxford University Press, 1960) pp. 118, 115.
31. Ward, "Land Use and Land Alienation," p. 12.
32. D.T. Lloyd, "Land Policy in Fiji," University of Cambridge Department of Land Economy, Occasional Paper No. 14 (1982), p. 143, sees such determination in favor of settler occupation and plantation use simply as resolution in equity; I see it more as a court-of-equity-like process that came to decisions at odds with the intent of that process.
33. Lands Claims Commission Final Report No. 1328, cited in Riles, "The Empty Place," p. 49.
34. Lloyd, "Land Policy in Fiji," p. 130.
35. France, Charter of the Land, p. 124.
36. Land Claims Commission Report No. 400, cited in Riles, "The Empty Place," p. 60. Robert Nicole, "The People Versus the Commission: Resistance to Land Registration in Fiji's Early Colonial History" University

of the South Pacific, 2014 http://repository.usp.ac.fj/9090/1/The_People_Versus_the_Commission_Robert_Nicole_PIURN_2014.pdf

37. Gaspard v. Colonial Sugar Refining Co. 3 Fiji Law Report 57, at 58. (Supreme Court of Fiji, 1904); Robert E. Nicole, "Disturbing History: Aspects of Resistance in Early Colonial Fiji," PhD dissertation, University of Canterbury, 2006, p. 196; Riles, "The Empty Place," p. 60.
38. Caldwell v. Mongston 2 Fiji Law Report 62 (Supreme Court of Fiji, 1908).
39. David Ress, *The Half Breed Tracts in Early National America: Changing Concepts of Land and Place* (New York: Palgrave Macmillan, 2019) pp. 77–102.
40. W.E. Maxwell, "The Laws and Customs of the Malays with Reference to the Tenure of Land," *Journal of the Royal Asiatic Society (Straits Branch)*, Vol. XIII (1884), p. 77.
41. Yeoh Seng Guan, "Creolized Utopias: Squatter Colonies and the Post-Colonial City in Malaysia," *Journal of Social Issues in Southeast Asia*, Vol. 16, No. 1 (April 2001), p. 106. Lim Teck Ghee. *Peasants and Their Agricultural Economy in Colonial Malaya, 1874–1940* (Kuala Lumpur: Oxford University Press, 1977).
42. S. Robert Aiken, "Losing Ground: Development, Natural Resources, and the Dispossession of Malaysia's Orang Asli," in *A History of Natural Resources in Asia: The Wealth of Nature*, edited by Greg Bankoff and Peter Boomgaard (New York: Palgrave Macmillan, 2007), pp. 174–177.
43. Adong bin Kuwau & Ors v Kerajaan Negeri Johor & Anor 1 MLJ 418, at 423–424, 426 (Mahkamah Persekutuan Malaysia, 1997).
44. Theodore B.F. Ruoff, *An Englishman Looks at the Torrens System: Being Some Provocative Essays on the Operation of the System after One Hundred Years* (Sydney: Law Book Company of Australia, 1957).
45. John L. McCormack, "Torrens and Recording: Land Title Assurance in the Computer Age," *William Mitchell Law Review*, Vol. 18 (1992), p. 101.
46. Rael v Taylor, 876 P.2d 1210 (Colorado Supreme Court, 1994) at 1213.
47. Ibid., at 1213–1214.
48. Costilla County Deed Book 1, p. 256, as cited by the court in Rael v Taylor at 1213.
49. Rael v. Taylor at 1214, 1215.
50. Sanchez v Taylor 377 F.2d 733 (10th U.S. Circuit of Appeals, 1967) at 737, 738–739.
51. Rael v Taylor at 1217.
52. *Ibid.*, at 1219.
53. Lobato v Taylor 71 P.3d 938 (Colorado Supreme Court. 2002).
54. In 1895 less than one-third of one percent of the land of England and Wales was on the Register. *Second and Final Report of the Royal Commission on the Land Transfer Acts, 1908–11* p. 11.

55. S. Rowton Simpson, *Land Law and Registration*, (Cambridge: Cambridge University Press, 1976) p. 88. The Torrens system was most commonly, but not universally, to record land title in Boston, Chicago and Minneapolis-St. Paul, Minnesota.
56. Percy Bordwell "The Resurrection of Registration of Title," *The University of Chicago Law Review*, Vol. 7, No. 3 (Apr., 1940), pp. 471, 482.
57. John T. Hassam, "Land Transfer Reform: The Australian System," *Harvard Law Review*, Vol. 4, No. 6 (Jan. 15, 1891), p. 273. Hassam supervised the indexing of Suffolk County (Boston) deed records.
58. M.M. Yeakle, *The Torrens System of Registration and Transfer of the Title to Real Estate* (Chicago: The Torrens Press, 1894), pp. 34, 45–46.
59. Myres S. McDougal and John W. Brabner-Smith, "Land Title Transfer: A Regression," *The Yale Law Journal*, Vol. 48, No. 7 (May, 1939), p. 1129.
60. Edward H. Cushman, "Torrens Titles and Title Insurance," *University of Pennsylvania Law Review and American Law Register*, Vol. 85, No. 6 (April, 1937) p. 606. To this point, see Partenfelder v. People, 211 N.Y. 355, 105 N.E. 675 (New York Supreme Court, 1914) and in re Sherman, 106 Misc. 244, 175 N.Y. Supp. 627 (New York Supreme Court, 1919).
61. Bordwell, "Resurrection of Registration," pp. 477–478; Richard R. Powell, *Registration of the Title to Land in the State of New York* (Rochester, N.Y.: Law Books Co., 1938) pp. 54–55.
62. Ernest Dowson and V.L.O. Sheppard, *Land Registration*, 2nd ed., HMSO Colonial Research Publications No. 13 (London: HMSO, 1956), p. 19.
63. D. Hall, P. Hirsch and T.M. Li, Powers of Exclusion: Land Dilemmas in Southeast Asia. (Singapore: NUS Press, 2011) pp: 27–9; T. Sikor and C. Lund, The Politics of Possession: Property, Authority, and Access to Natural Resources (Chichester: Wiley-Blackwell, 2009), p. 1.
64. Joseph H. Beale, "Registration of Title to Land," *Harvard Law Review*, Vol. 6, No. 7 (15 Feb. 1893), p. 369.
65. Toro v Kiri, VUSC 210 (Vanuatu Supreme Court, 2013).
66. Rufford G. Patton and Carroll G. Patton, *Patton on Titles* (St. Paul: West, 1957) p. 17.
67. James P. Root, "An Abstract of Title," *The American Law Register*, Vol. 23, No. 9, New Series Volume 14 (Sep., 1875), p. 539.
68. *Ibid.*, pp. 532–533.
69. J.F. Bullitt letter in "The Torrens System: An Open Symposium," *The Virginia Law Register*, Vol. 11, No. 7 (Nov., 1905), p. 595.

References

Adong bin Kuwau & Ors v Kerajaan Negeri Johor & Anor 1 MLJ 418, at 423–424, 426 (Mahkamah Persekutuan Malaysia, 1997).

Caldwell v. Mongston 2 Fiji Law Report 62 (Supreme Court of Fiji, 1908).
Gaspard v. Colonial Sugar Refining Co. 3 Fiji Law Report 57, at 58. (Supreme Court of Fiji, 1904).
Lobato v Taylor 71 P.3d 938 (Colorado Supreme Court. 2002).
Mateo Cariño v. Insular Government of the Philippine Islands. 7 Phil 132, (Philippines Supreme Court, 1906).
Mateo Cariño v. Insular Government of the Philippine Islands 212 U.S. 449 (U.S. Supreme Court, 1909).
Notes of the Proceedings of a Native Council 1876.
——— 1878.
Rael v Taylor, 876 P.2d 1210 (Colorado Supreme Court, 1994).
Sanchez v Taylor 377 F.2d 733 (10th U.S. Circuit of Appeals,1967).
Second and Final Report of the Royal Commission on the Land Transfer Acts, 1908–11.
in re Sherman, 106 Misc. 244, 175 N. Y. Supp. 627 (New York Supreme Court, 1919).
State ex rel. Attorney Gen. v. Guilbert, 56 Ohio St. 575 (Ohio Supreme Court, 1897).
Toro v Kiri, VUSC 210 (Vanuatu Supreme Court, 2013).
Tyler v. Judges of the Court of Registration 151 Mass. 71 (Supreme Judicial Court of Massachusetts, 1900).
Tyler v. Judges of the Court of Registration, 179 U.S. 405 (U.S. Supreme Court, 1900).
Webster v Reid 52 U.S. 437 (U.S. Supreme Court, 1850).
Aiken, S. Robert. 2007. Losing Ground: Development, Natural Resources, and the Dispossession of Malaysia's Orang Asli. In *A History of Natural Resources in Asia: The Wealth of Nature*, ed. Greg Bankoff and Peter Boomgaard. New York: Palgrave Macmillan.
Beale, Joseph H. 1893. Registration of Title to Land. *Harvard Law Review* 6 (7): 369–377.
Blackstone, William. 1979 [1765]. *Commentaries on the Laws of England*. Chicago: University of Chicago.
Bordwell, Percy. 1940. The Resurrection of Registration of Title. *The University of Chicago Law Review* 7 (3): 470–488.
Bullitt, J.F. 1905. Letter in "The Torrens System: An Open Symposium". *The Virginia Law Register* 11 (7): 595.
Cushman, Edward H. 1937. Torrens Titles and Title Insurance. *University of Pennsylvania Law Review and American Law Register* 85 (6): 589–612.
Dowson, Ernest, and V.L.O. Sheppard. 1956. *Land Registration*. 2nd ed, HMSO Colonial Research Publications No. 13. London: HMSO.
Fison, Lorimer. 1881. *Land Tenure in Fiji*. London: Harrison.
France, Peter. 1960. *Charter of the Land: Custom and Colonisation in Fiji*. Oxford: Oxford University Press.

Ghee, Lim Teck. 1977. *Peasants and Their Agricultural Economy in Colonial Malaya, 1874–1940*. Kuala Lumpur: Oxford University Press.
Guan, Yeoh Seng. April 2001. Creolized Utopias: Squatter Colonies and the Post-Colonial City in Malaysia. *Journal of Social Issues in Southeast Asia* 16 (1): 102–124.
Habana, Olivia M. 2000. Gold Mining in Benguet to 1898. *Philippine Studies* 48 (4): 455–487.
Hall, D., P. Hirsch, and T.M. Li. 2011. *Powers of Exclusion: Land Dilemmas in Southeast Asia*. Singapore: NUS Press.
Harvey, Eustace J. 1910. *Land Law and Registration of Title, A Comparison of the Old and New Ways of Transferring Land*. London: Longmans, Green & Co.
Hassam, John T. 1891. Land Transfer Reform: The Australian System. *Harvard Law Review* 4 (6): 271–279.
Hogg, James Edward. 1920. *Registration of Title to Land throughout the Empire: A Treatise on the Law Relating to Warranty of Title to Land by Registration and Transactions with Registered Land in Australia, New Zealand, Canada, England, Ireland, West Indies, Malaya, etc.* Carswell: Toronto.
Ibaloi Chieftan Descendents Assail NCIP. 2010. *The Philippines Star*, February 12.
Ibaloi Family Cries Foul over Land Claim Mess. 2010. *Philippines Daily Inquirer*, February 13.
Ibrahim, Tan Sri Datuk Professor Ahmad and Judith Sihombing. 1989. *The Centenary of the Torrens System in Malaysia*. Singapore/Kuala Lumpur: Malayan Law Journal.
Kane, S.E. 1933. *Life and Death in Luzon or Thirty Years with the Philippine Head-Hunters*. New York: Grosset & Dunlap.
Knapman, Bruce. 1987. *Fiji's Economic History, 1874–1939: Studies of Capitalist Colonial Development*. Canberra: National Centre for Development Studies, Research School of Pacific Studies, Australian National University.
Lloyd, D.T. 1982. Land Policy in Fiji. University of Cambridge Department of Land Economy, Occasional Paper No. 14.
Maxwell, W.E. 1884. The Laws and Customs of the Malays with Reference to the Tenure of Land. *Journal of the Royal Asiatic Society (Straits Branch)* XIII: 43–220.
McCormack, John L. 1992. Torrens and Recording: Land Title Assurance in the Computer Age. *William Mitchell Law Review* 18 (1): 61–129.
McDougal, Myres S., and John W. Brabner-Smith. 1939. Land Title Transfer: A Regression. *The Yale Law Journal* 48 (7): 1125–1151.
Milking What's Left of the Baguio Dairy Farm. 2016. *Philippines Daily Inquirer*, August 17.
Nicole, Robert E. 2006. Disturbing History: Aspects of Resistance in Early Colonial Fiji. PhD dissertation, University of Canterbury.

Nicole, Robert. 2014. The People Versus the Commission: Resistance to Land Registration in Fiji's Early Colonial History. University of the South Pacific. http://repository.usp.ac.fj/9090/1/The_People_Versus_the_Commission_Robert_Nicole_PIURN_2014.pdf

Patton, Rufford G., and Carroll G. Patton. 1957. *Patton on Titles*. St. Paul: West.

Powell, Richard R. 1938. *Registration of the Title to Land in the State of New York*. Rochester: Law Books Co.

Pritchard, W.T. 1866. *Polynesian Reminiscences; or, Life in the South Pacific Islands*. London: Chapman, & Hall.

Ress, David. 2019. *The Half Breed Tracts in Early National America: Changing Concepts of Land and Place*. New York: Palgrave Macmillan.

Riles, Annelise. 2003. The Empty Place: Legal Formalities and the Cultural State. In *The Place of Law*, ed. Austin Sarat, Lawrence Douglas, and Martha Merrill Umphrey, 43–73. Ann Arbor: University of Michigan Press.

Root, James P. 1875. An Abstract of Title. *The American Law Register* 23 (9)., New Series Volume 14: 529–543.

Rose, Carol. 1994. *Property and Persuasion: Essays on the History, Theory, and Rhetoric of Ownership*. Boulder: Westview Press.

Ruoff, Theodore B.F. 1957. *An Englishman Looks at the Torrens System: Being Some Provocative Essays on the Operation of the System After One Hundred Years*. Sydney: Law Book Company of Australia.

Sikor, T., and C. Lund. 2009. *The Politics of Possession: Property, Authority, and Access to Natural Resources*. Chichester: Wiley-Blackwell.

Simpson, S. Rowton. 1976. *Land Law and Registration*. Cambridge: Cambridge University Press.

The Benguet Consolidated Mining Co. 1936. *Port of Manila and Other Phillippine Ports Year Book*, 23. Manila: Manila Harbor Board.

Torrens, Robert Richard. 1882. *An Essay on the Transfer of Land by Registration, Under the Duplicate Method Operative in British Colonies*. London: Cassell, Petter, Galpin & Co.

Ward, Gerald R. 1969. Land Use and Land Alienation in Fiji to 1885. *Journal of Pacific History* 4: 3–25.

Yeakle, M.M. 1894. *The Torrens System of Registration and Transfer of the Title to Real Estate*. Chicago: The Torrens Press.

CHAPTER 6

Conclusion

Abstract Both deed recordation on the Massachusetts model and Torrens land title registration transformed what had long been a private matter (both in terms of law and of socio-economic relations) into matters of state. This was a consequence of the uncertainties that arose with (a) the settlement of land that was supposed to be unoccupied but that in fact belonged to another group and (b) the supposed irrelevance in a new colony of familiar European notions of use rights and a limited landed class. Both systems reflected and reinforced the new ideas that land was like any other capital asset, that its value derived from what it would fetch in a marketplace rather than its natural endowments, and that the fee simple package of land rights—including freedom to sell, to waste, and to exclude others—was fundamental to human nature and human progress. The historical context of the introduction and evolution of recordation and registration, however, suggests that this is not the case.

Keywords Deed recordation • Land title registration • Torrens system • Land market

For, in the end, recordation on the Massachusetts model and title registration in Torrens' system are both about an alliance with power. Power, to be sure, is what ownership of land has always been about, for those exclusive rights to possess, to occupy, and use depended on the power to

D. Ress, *Deeds, Titles, and Changing Concepts of Land Rights*, https://doi.org/10.1007/978-3-030-64191-7_6

exclude—power that could be exercised in the very rawest way, by force. In the stories of seventeenth and eighteenth century legal theory, the earliest apportioning of land came when individuals simply took it and held it by the exercise of whatever power they might personally bring to bear. So, for instance, where the fringe of Illinois forest met the prairie, a squatter's rifle might secure a farmstead—or an intruder's quicker trigger finger might effect a transfer. Recordation and registration merely invoke institutions of the state in asserting the particular rights—to exclude, to waste, and to sell—that are embodied in ownership.

Both systems invoked the state because they memorialized rights of ownership on land to which others, individuals, and groups who were outside the state believed they had conflicting rights to land. While the earliest recorded deeds granted by New England's Native peoples to the English settlers might sometimes try to recognize shared English and Native rights on a piece of land, such a coexistence of rights was difficult to set down on paper. This was the case whether the text was in English or in Massachusett; it was the case, as the very wording of the deeds themselves suggests, because neither grantor nor grantee had narrowly fixed ideas about the rights to land that they wished to secure. That later deeds, and Torrens's title certificates, were clearer reflects a profound shift in what the people creating those documents wanted to accomplish.

Ideas about land and about the place of people on land were changing as new commercial and industrial practices took hold on either side of the Atlantic. The early nineteenth century American economist Francis Wayland would stress the importance of a public record of landholding, so that it might be passed on to the next generation. Jeremy Bentham declared that the value of a piece land reflected certainty of tenure. The emerging idea was that value depended not on stewardship but on the power to transform—and to sell. "What are called natural advantages, like fertile soils are dependent for their value wholly upon the application of labour and capital," the American economist Henry Carey wrote. To make this point, he noted that coal when still underground "has all the qualities it possesses when it is brought into use in New York or Philadelphia, yet acres of land containing thousands of tons may be purchased for fifty cents" while people paid $50 to $100 an acre "for little more than a bed of sand in New Jersey" since "It is cheaper for them to pay for the use of capital employed in bringing water and coal to them, than to go and seek them where they may be had gratis."[1]

Land where people might once have felt they and their descendants could be permanently rooted, whether because they formally owned it or simply had customary rights to live on it, had become something less than simply a place to live and work upon. Something, that is, with which they had only a temporary connection. Something that instead of yielding a way of life could, for those individuals who happened to have a recognized title to land, yield most importantly a monetary gain. For Robert Richard Torrens, the basic problem with the English land law that he hoped to overturn with his South Australian registration system was that it made buying and selling land—that is, to create or sever that temporary connection—too complicated and costly.

While the ability to sell land was not an innovation of commercial and industrial societies, it had long been common for laws and custom to regulate or constrain the transfer or encumbering of land. It was not until the rise of capitalist commodity and financial markets emerged, accompanied by an idealizing of their function, that land sales accelerated to the point of poisoning the relationships that people in traditional communities had established, Karl Polanyi argues.[2] In the United States, where calls to end entail and primogeniture were important elements in Revolutionary Era argument for separation from an aristocratic British, a series of state statutes and court decisions had by the mid-nineteenth century eroded the tradition of passing family landholdings on through the generations by declaring that creditors' claims came first, as Claire Priest notes.[3]

Australians, too, saw easy commerce in land with titles uncomplicated by other claims (beyond those of the creditors with loans secured by land for the purchase or improvement of land) as an essential element of democratic society. "The working men of New South Wales are almost all becoming landed proprietors; but hardly one of them would ever attend a sale of land if it were not announced in the advertisement 'that the title was that of Torrens' Act,'" as legislative council member Thomas Holt was widely quoted though the 1880s.[4] The benefits to South Australia from Torrens' system came "chiefly by restoring to its intrinsic value a large amount of property depreciated or unmarketable through defective evidence or technical imperfection in title," in one Victorian journalist's view. This editor concluded that "a cheap, simple expeditious and accurate system of transfer of land would boost its price by the equivalent of four to ten years' rent" (a common way of calculating a value for land in England).[5] Buying and selling, in short, was the point of both deed recordation and Torrens' title, as Carol Rose noted when she described them as setting "crystalline rules for the sake of simplicity and ease of land sales and purchases."[6]

The point is not that land sales were a new phenomenon of capitalism, but rather that the enormous increase in the number and ease of transactions facilitated by the view that markets know best had turned land into a financial asset like any other. Land, and the paper that recorded its status, was like the shares of stock that, as Harvard Law professor Joseph Beale said, were a model for dealing in land under the Torrens system. The recorded deeds in an American court house or the land title certificates in the care of a government registrar were, like the warrants that created virtual land in Kentucky, an abstract representation of a physical reality that had the power to change the nature of that reality. Land could be something other than a home or farmstead; it could become an investment, where what was valuable was not that secured you a place to live, but a chance to make a profitable deal.

It was a sense that the scale of commerce in land had become overwhelming, after all, that prompted the attorney John T. Hassam to call for adoption of Torrens' system in Massachusetts. He bemoaned the fact that while records from Boston's first century filled just 19 record books, records from the city's third century, the 1800s, filled more than 1700.[7] Dealings in land proceeded apace in either system. While "Land is the source of all material wealth," the barrister and former Sudan Political Service official Rowton Simpson cautioned that "Land registration must, however, be kept in perspective … It is not some sort of magical specific which will automatically produce good land use and development; nor is it a system of land holding."[8]

The functioning of one perhaps not completely magical specific—the market in real estate—cared little about whether rights to land were declared by recording deeds or state certification of title through registration. The economist William Stanley Jevons, shortly after returning to England from New South Wales, argued that a registry was not needed in Britain, since the cost of any more cumbersome system "would show itself in the price … in proportion than other investments offering an equally certain return."[9] The rational actors who made Jevons' analysis of value, investment, and the distribution of income work, that is, would buy land when it yielded a percentage return on the purchase price that matched or exceeded the return from some other type of capital good—a ship, perhaps (as the economist Willard Phillips might have said), or machine tool or factory. In the end, Jevons would eventually conclude:

> If land yields an annual revenue of corn and wool, milk, beef, and other necessaries, houses yield a revenue of shelter and comfort. The sole end of all industry is to satisfy our wants; and if capital is requisite to supply shelter, and furniture and useful utensils, as it undoubtedly is, why refuse it the name which it bears in all other employments?[10]

Torrens tried to half-heartedly rebut this by arguing that Jevons ignored "the feeling of exhilaration which most men experience when treading on their own land" as well as the status that comes with ownership and pleasures of working on the land. "These compensate the yeoman and the squire for the heavy costs and uncertainties of conveyancing, as well as for the lower rate of interest than stock or railway debentures would afford him," Torrens argued.[11] To be sure, whether the argument is that the cost of transfer is reflected in the price of land when compared to other capital goods offering similar returns, or whether the cost is compensated for by other, non-financial measures, the conclusion to be drawn from both opponent and proponent of Torrens's system is that variation in mechanics of declaring ownership did not diminish interest in owning land.

It was, after all, difficult to see any other connection people might have to land by the time Torrens made his point. And it was difficult in part because the public paperwork detailing the status of any particular piece of land was no longer declaring any relationship other than ownership. Even the recorded deeds in which Colorado Territorial Governor Gilpin had so carefully tried to protect longstanding rights of use and access to the commons of the San Luis Valley could not counter the simpler rights embodied in a Torrens title for many decades. When newcomers in the 1800s began encroaching on the commons of open field arable, pastures and woods set up by the first permanent settlers at the mouth of the Missouri river in the eighteenth century, the Recorder of Deeds in St. Louis struggled to understand the nature of their rights. The villagers of Carondolet, Missouri, had to petition Congress for help, writing that "we have been for upwards of Thirty years in peaceful possession of a Certain Quantity of Land as Commons … which Commons always was & still is the only support of ourselves & our families being our only Dependance for Building our houses, Fencing our Cornfields, our Firewood & Pasture for our Stock." In the end, it would require a directive from the chief of the US General Land Office to protect those shared spaces.[12] Eventually, Missouri state legislators simply wrote a law declaring that the commons belonged to the several now-incorporated river towns rather than simply to the people who lived by them and used them.[13] In 1870s England where deeds were still a private matter between buyer and seller, it took an act of Parliament to set down in writing a compromise that the Earl Spencer and the villagers of Wimbledon reached to preserve the commons on land he owned, they could use and on which others were beginning to encroach. (Parliament set up a Board of Conservators to keep the commons unenclosed and in a natural state, ending commons rights of cutting turf, taking wood and digging gravel and clay that had been disfiguring the land and putting an end to Spencer's plan to subdivide it and sell house lots.)[14]

Trespass, and the possibility of trespass, will lead people to declare their rights (or their supposed rights) to land for all to see, whether in Carondolet, Missouri, or Wimbledon, South West London. Why else, after all, post "No Trespassing" notices along the boundaries of your land? But trespassing had long seemed more a private matter than a public one. In one of the few published rulings by nineteenth century American courts on trespassing, Virginia's Supreme Court held in 1837 that trespassing was not a crime in common law. Laws dating back to colonial days and some new state Constitutions of the 1770s said hunters might freely pursue game on unenclosed land.[15] To ask the town to record your right to land, as Mr. Rowle did, or to take the additional step that Torrens convinced South Australia to take and certify individuals' ownership of land, made trespass a public matter at precisely these moments when two different peoples, with two different ways of living on the land, raised the question of who had what rights to which land.

Oftentimes, the answer to this question comes simply from force of arms—both American and Australian histories are full of accounts of war and massacre in contests over land and its produce. But seventeenth century Massachusetts, where deed recordation starts, and mid-nineteenth century South Australia, where Torrens launched his system, share some significant features. In both, the myth that colonists had arrived at an empty land was impossible to sustain. In both, a different myth, that colonists might lead the indigenous people of those not empty lands to share the newcomers' way of life, reflected the distinctive religious and moral sensibilities of a significant portion of the earliest settlers. And in both, the colonists' own ideas of the proper relationship of individuals and land were not completely settled.

The careful reservation of fishing, foraging, and hunting rights noted in the deeds that Mr. Rowle and his English and Pennacook neighbors recorded suggest it was not uncommon for public proclamation of land rights to recognized share claims and to try to regulate potential conflicts of rights. This remained a function of recorded deeds for many decades, as with one in 1708 when Martha Lord turned over her house and orchard at nearby Mount Misery as well as 65 acres along the Great Works River to her son Benjamin. Her deed recording that made clear that she granted "full power to grant bargain Sell and convey the Same" as well as his promise not to interfere with her as she remained in the house in exchange for an annual rent of corn, cider, and £4.[16] The United Illinois and Wabash Companies and its opponents in the US government argued for nearly a half century for the validity of a 1773 deed for hundreds of thousands of acres along the Mississippi, Ohio, and Illinois rivers. To make their cases, both the company and the government would at different times assert that the Illiniwek chiefs who granted the land owned the land, if they thought that view would bolster an argument. At other points, each argued that the chiefs were simply agents of the individuals who actually owned the land, either collectively or individually. The deed itself declared that the 22 partners in the United Companies, rather than the company itself, acquired the land in severalty—that is, defying logic, that the 22 individuals each had separate and individual rights to possess the undivided land, and that each of those 22 separate and exclusive rights were not shared with any other person. In the end, in the landmark case Johnson v M'Intosh, US Supreme Court Justice John Marshall ruled that Native Americans did not have the kind of rights to land that allowed them to sell land to individuals. They could only cede their land to the government, whether after conquest or by some notionally voluntary act.[17]

None of these deeds, not Mr. Rowle's, Mrs. Lord's, nor the United Companies, reflect the property rights legal scholars' view that ownership meant right of exclusive use that theories of capital and of law deemed essential before land could be made productive. Ownership as an absolute right to exclude and waste and sell was not seen as a necessary or urgent matter. New Jersey and Connecticut never got around to declaring land ownership would be allodial—free of any superior claim—until 14 and 17 years after independence.[18] The sense that Australian pastoralists or American cattle kings might let their stock freely range, or that chasing a deer through a neighbor's field was not a trespass, suggests there was still a notion that land was to be shared. This notion would lead to the preservation of Wimbledon's common. It led to creation of public parks, beginning with the first state park, Georgia's Indian Springs, in 1832, and later with the first national parks, Yellowstone, established in 1872, and the

Royal National Park outside Sydney in 1879. The old idea that working on the land created a property right to it was still a deeply held belief into the middle of the nineteenth century, expressed every time a squatter staked his claim to a farmstead by blazing trees and staking posts or a lumberjack took down a tree from someone else's unpatrolled land.

Recordation and registration grew from uncertainty over rights to land. This was an uncertainty that came in part because emigrants to new colonies arrived there to find other people with their own ideas about land and in part because those emigrants left a country where they had not owned land and so had no direct knowledge of what the rights of owners actually entailed. What they did know was that they needed to secure a right to occupy and use land. What they discovered was that recordation and registration, in addition to proclaiming those rights, also facilitated buying and selling land. Technique intended to attack uncertainty became tools to reinforce a particular way of thinking about land that was on the ascent and that was pushing aside alternative notions about other ways people might find their place upon the land.

But land and the people who belong to it lose something when land becomes mere capital or, those even greater abstractions: a square on a cadastral map, an entry in a registry or page in a deed book, the asset underlying a derivative like the scrip that disposed of the lands of the Half Breed Tracts of Minnesota and Nebraska. And the supposed gains—better and larger crops of food and fiber, rational exploitation of timber and minerals and grazing lands—are not necessarily evident away from the pages of economics texts. The introduction of Torrens' title registration in British and American colonial territories has meant individuals whose political connections and place a state or village power structure give them easier access to the registrars end up with land. Often, they will get land where they never had any kind of connection. They will win an ownership right that entitles them to a claim on the income that the individuals who still actually live on and work the land. Even when the person who actually works on the land receives a title to it, registration is at least as likely to lead to dispossession as to investment; as Rowton Simpson commented after reviewing land registration operations in Africa and the Punjab, "There is no surer way to deprive a peasant of his land than to give him a registered title which is freely negotiated as a bank note."[19]

Here, perhaps, it is time to be explicit. The history of recordation and registration, with origins in colonies created by the dispossession of indigenous peoples, ought to make us question whether human progress and human liberty inevitably require the rights that come with ownership. A history that shows the earliest recorded deeds regulated potential conflicts over rights to land rights ought to remind us that we have known ways to accommodate other modes of living on and with the land. The history that followed of simplifying deeds and searches, and of introducing state certification of fee simple ownership, made it easier to erase others' rights to be on land and enjoy its bounty—and so might lead us to wonder if perhaps what buyers and sellers gained was worth the cost. As might a look at some of the consequences that come when land is simply another bit of capital to finance and use up.

In the history of recordation and registration we might just find a reminder that we have the power, through the law and the language that it uses, to find better ways of living on the land. We might find that what Mr. Rowle wanted—a better life for his children and their children on the land that they belonged to—is what is possible for all of us to attain, if we only manage to convince our neighbors to set it down somewhere as a promise to the world at large.

Notes

1. Henry Carey, *Principles of Political Economy*, (Philadelphia: Carey, Lea & Blanchard, 1837) pp. 21, 46, 131.
2. Karl Polanyi, *The Great Transformation: The Political and Economic Origins of Our Time* (Boston: Beacon, 2001 [1944]) espy. pp. 71–80.
3. Claire Priest, "Creating an American Property Law: Alienability and Its Limits in American History," *Harvard Law Review*, Vol. 120, No. 2 (December, 2006), p. 457.
4. *The Remedy for Landlordism* (London: Keegan, Paul, Trench & Co., 1889) p. 66.
5. Frederick Sinnett, *An Account of the Colony of South Australia* (Adelaide: W.C. Cox, 1862) p. 99.
6. Carol Rose, "Crystals and Mud in Property Law," *Stanford Law Review*, Vol. 40, No. 3 (February, 1988), p. 589.
7. John Hassam, "Land Transfer Reform: The Australian System," *Harvard Law Review*, Vol. 4, No. 6 (January, 1891) p. 273.
8. S. Rowton Simpson, *Land Law and Registration* (Cambridge: Cambridge University Press, 1976) p. 3.
9. William Stanley Jevons comments cited in Robert Richard Torrens, *An Essay on the Transfer of Land by Registration* (London: Cassell, Petter,

Galpin & Co., 1882) pp. 27–28, quoting Jevons's article on registration in *The Fortnightly*, March 1881.

10. William Stanley Jevons, *The Theory of Political Economy* (London: Macmillan, 1888) 3rd edition, p. 200.
11. Robert Richard Torrens, *An Essay on the Transfer of Land by Registration, under the Duplicate Method Operative in British Colonies* (London: Cassell, Petter, Galpin & Co., 1882), p. 37.
12. "Petition of the Inhabitants of Carondolet" January 8 1817 in Territorial Papers of the United States. Clarence Edwin Carter, editor Vol. 15 (Washington: Government Printing Office, 1951) p. 241; Josiah Meigs to Edward Hempstead, March 11 1817, Ibid., p. 252.
13. "An Act concerning Commons" (1824), in Laws of the State of Missouri, Vol. 1, p. 211.
14. Wimbledon and Putney Commons Act, Anno 34 & 35, Victoriae Reginae, Cap. XXIV. Section 34 requires the whole of the commons remain unenclosed, section 36 that they be maintained in their natural aspect, and section 37 ends commons rights of cutting turf, taking wood and digging gravel or clay.
15. Commonwealth v. Powell, 8 Leigh, 719 (Virginia Supreme Court, 1837).
16. York County, Maine, Deed Book VII, folio 125.
17. *American State Papers, Public Lands*, Vol. 2, p. 97.
18. An Act concerning Tenures, 18 February 1795, *New Jersey Revised Laws*, Trenton, 1821, p. 166; Act of 1798, Title 56, Ch. 1 Section 1, *Connecticut Revised Statutes*, Hartford, 1821.
19. S. Rowton Simpson, "New land law in Malawi," *Journal of Administration Overseas* Vol. 6, No.4, (1967) p. 227; Siobhan McDonnell, "Urban Land Grabbing by Political Elites: Exploring the Political Economy of Land and the Challenges of Regulation, in Siobham McDonnell, Matthew G. Allen, and Colin Filer, editors, *Kastom, property and ideology: Land transformations in Melanesia* (Canberra: ANU Press, 2017) pp 283–305; P. Shipton, "Debts and trespasses: land, mortgages, and the ancestors in western Kenya," *Africa* Vol. 62, No.3, (1992) pp. 357–388; Catherine Besteman, "Individualisation and the Assault on Customary Tenure in Africa: Title Registration Programmes and the Case of Somalia," Africa: Journal of the International African Institute, Vol. 64, No. 4 (1994), pp. 484–515; M. Goheen, "Land accumulation and local control: the manipulation of symbols and power in Nso, Cameroon," in R. Downs and S. Reyna (eds.), *Land and Society in Contemporary Africa*, pp. 280–308. Hanover, N.H.: University Press of New England, 1988).

References

An Act concerning Commons, in *Laws of the State of Missouri*, 1824.

An Act concerning Tenures, 18 February 1795, *New Jersey Revised Laws*, 1821.

Act of 1798, Title 56, Ch. 1 Section 1, *Connecticut Revised Statutes*, 1821.

Commonwealth v. Powell, 8 Leigh, 719 (Virginia Supreme Court, 1837).

Wimbledon and Putney Commons Act, Anno 34 & 35, Victoriae Reginae, Cap. XXIV. Section 34.

York County, Maine, Deed Book VI.

The Remedy for Landlordism (London: Keegan, Paul, Trench & Co., 1889).

Besteman, Catherine. 1994. Individualisation and the Assault on Customary Tenure in Africa: Title Registration Programmes and the Case of Somalia. *Africa: Journal of the International African Institute* 64 (4): 484–515.

Carey, Henry. 1837. *Principles of Political Economy*. Philadelphia: Carey, Lea & Blanchard.

Goheen, M. 1988. Land Accumulation and Local Control: The Manipulation of Symbols and Power in Nso, Cameroon. In *Land and Society in Contemporary Africa*, ed. R. Downs and S. Reyna, 280–308. Hanover: University Press of New England.

Hassam, John. 1891. Land Transfer Reform: The Australian System. *Harvard Law Review* 4 (6): 271–279.

Jevons, William Stanley. 1888. *The Theory of Political Economy*. London: Macmillan.

McDonnell, Siobhan. 2017. Urban Land Grabbing by Political Elites: Exploring the Political Economy of Land and the Challenges of Regulation. In *Kastom, Property and Ideology: Land Transformations in Melanesia*, ed. Siobham McDonnell, Matthew G. Allen, and Colin Filer, 283–305. Canberra: ANU Press.

Polanyi, Karl. 2001 [1944]. *The Great Transformation: The Political and Economic Origins of Our Time*. Boston: Beacon.

Priest, Claire. 2006. Creating an American Property Law: Alienability and Its Limits in American History. *Harvard Law Review*, Vol. 120 (2): 385–459.

Rose, Carol. 1988. Crystals and Mud in Property Law. *Stanford Law Review* 40 (3): 577–610.

Shipton, P. 1992. Debts and Trespasses: Land, Mortgages, and the Ancestors in Western Kenya. *Africa* 62 (3): 357–388.

Simpson, S. Rowton. 1976. *Land Law and Registration*. Cambridge: Cambridge University Press.

———. 1967. New Land Law in Malawi. *Journal of Administration Overseas* 6 (4): 221–228.

Sinnett, Frederick. 1862. *An Account of the Colony of South Australia*. Adelaide: W.C. Cox.
Torrens, Robert Richard. 1882. *An Essay on the Transfer of Land by Registration*. London, Cassell, Petter, Galpin & Co.
———. 1859. *The South Australian System of Conveyancing by Registration of Title*. Register and Observer: Adelaide.

Index[1]

[1] Note: Page numbers followed by 'n' refer to notes.

D. Ress, *Deeds, Titles, and Changing Concepts of Land Rights*,
https://doi.org/10.1007/978-3-030-64191-7

The manufacturer's authorised representative in the EU is Springer Nature Customer Service Centre GmbH, Europaplatz 3, 69115 Heidelberg, Germany. If you have any concerns regarding our products, please contact ProductSafety@springernature.com

Printed and bound by CPI Group (UK) Ltd, Croydon, CR0 4YY
22/09/2026
02221054-0017

Assessing Health Care